Scoundrels
and
Scallywags

Scoundrels *and* Scallywags

CHARACTERS FROM ALBERTA'S PAST

Brian Brennan

FIFTH
HOUSE

Cover photograph, William "Wild Bill" Peyto, Glenbow Archives NA-1438-1
Cover background photograph by Alec Pytlowany / Masterfile
Cover and interior design by John Luckhurst / GDL

The publisher gratefully acknowledges the support of
The Canada Council for the Arts and the Department of Canadian Heritage.

THE CANADA COUNCIL   LE CONSEIL DES ARTS
FOR THE ARTS   DU CANADA
SINCE 1957   DEPUIS 1957

We acknowledge the financial support of the Government of Canada through the Book Publishing Industry Development Program for our publishing activities.

Printed in Canada by Transcontinental Printing.

02 03 04 05 06 / 5 4 3 2 1

First published in the United States in 2003.

National Library of Canada Cataloguing in Publication Data

Brennan, Brian, 1943-
    Scoundrels and scallywags

    Includes index.
    ISBN 1-894004-92-2

    1. Alberta--Biography. 2. Alberta--History--Miscellanea. I. Title.
FC3655.B736 2002   920.07123   C2002-911002-5
F1075.8.B73 2002

Fifth House Ltd.   In the United States:
A Fitzhenry & Whiteside Company   Fitzhenry & Whiteside
1511-1800 4 St. SW   121 Harvard Avenue, Suite 2
Calgary, Alberta, Canada   Allston, MA
T2S 2S5   02134

1-800-387-9776
www.fitzhenry.ca

To Zelda and Nicole
my beloved companions on the journey

AND TO

Maud and Jack
who gave me the wings to fly

Contents

Introduction

We can't give them knighthoods, like the English have done with such bad-boy rockers as Sir Mick Jagger and Sir Elton John—in Alberta we like to honour our scoundrels and scallywags in other ways. Nowhere is this more evident than in Fort McMurray, where a street and a shopping mall are named after Peter Pond, an eighteenth-century American adventurer, fur trader, and confessed murderer forced to leave the Athabasca region in 1788 after the death of a fur-trading opponent named John Ross. As writer Aritha van Herk perceptively observed, Peter Pond "fits right into the tradition of this province, long before anyone could have predicted the maverick place it would become."

John Rowand, who today is commemorated at Edmonton's historic Fort Edmonton Park, was another white hustler who caught the scrappy spirit of Alberta long before it was declared a province of Canada in 1905. A burly Hudson's Bay Company factor who ruled with his temper and his fists, the scoundrelly Rowand controlled a huge fur-trading empire for thirty years from his palatial headquarters at Fort Edmonton. He was characterized admiringly by his boss—the Hudson's Bay governor Sir George Simpson—as "one of the most pushing, bustling men in the service."

Another park in Edmonton honours the misguided William Hawrelak, the eternal boomerang of Alberta municipal politics, twice forced to quit the mayor's office because of questionable land dealings. A provincial building is named after the indiscreet John Brownlee, the disgraced premier who left office after a jury convicted him of seducing a twenty-two-year-old government secretary. In Calgary, the tradition of giving white hats to visiting celebrities is done in the name of blustering Don Mackay, an ardent civic booster and municipal politician who lost his job as mayor after it was revealed that he had used thirty-five bags of city-owned cement to pour the basement of his holiday home in Banff. In the Rocky

Mountains, a peak is named after Wild Bill Peyto, a legendary prospector and trapper who, it is said, once let a lynx loose in a Banff saloon just to see how quickly the drunken patrons could get to their feet. Another peak is named after General Thomas Strange, an eccentric British army officer who led a ragtag force of Alberta cowboys, scouts, and mounted police to fight in the Riel Rebellion. In Blairmore, a left-leaning town council once voted to rename the town's main street in honour of Tim Buck, the one-time leader of the Communist Party of Canada. There's no evidence that Buck ever actually lived in Alberta, but he was a popular speaker at miners' meetings in Canmore and the Crowsnest Pass during the 1920s and 1930s.

I have been drawn to these people who dared to live outside the boundaries of convention ever since I arrived in Alberta in 1974. When I worked as a journalist in Calgary, I always found it more interesting to write about a fringe mayoralty candidate like the convicted felon Jimmy "the Con" Carleton or about the malapropism-spouting alderman John Kushner, than about the more sober, more earnest figures on the local public scene. The latter undoubtedly did good works for their community, but they always seemed, even on colour television, to be tinted in various shades of grey.

Some readers may wonder about the selection criteria I used for the people profiled in this book. What brings a loud and abrasive but otherwise inoffensive alderman like Edmonton's Julia Kiniski together with a convicted murderer like Emilio Picariello, or a doomed country singer like Tommy Common, or a determined hate-monger like the Ku Klux Klan leader John James Maloney? Who are the "scoundrels" and who are the "scallywags"? And what exactly is a "scallywag"? Well, here's where you can have some fun with the language, because "scallywag" happens to be one of those delightfully enigmatic words that Humpty Dumpty might have been thinking about when he said to Alice in *Through the Looking Glass*, "When I use a word, it means just what I choose it to mean—neither more nor less."

Nobody seems to know for sure where the word "scallywag" first came from or what its etymology might be. "Nineteenth century U.S. slang of unknown origin," says my *Concise Oxford Dictionary* brusquely. It defines the word (with alternative spellings of "scalawag" and "scallawag") as a "good-for-nothing person, scamp or scapegrace." Another dictionary defines "scallywag" as a "rascal or rogue." I'm rather partial to that last definition myself because it inspired our stage name when a friend and I toured Canada in the 1960s, singing Irish parlour songs and calling ourselves the Dublin Rogues.

As examples in this book of scallywags—rascally or roguish or eccentric individuals who resisted being stereotyped, domesticated, branded, ignored, or taxed—I would draw your attention to the charming story of the rancher from Priddis, Fred Perceval, who decided he would prefer to live in obscurity among cattle and horses in the grasslands of southern Alberta rather than ascend to the House of Lords when he became England's eleventh Earl of Egmont. Or consider the chutzpah of gregarious cowboy showman Guy Weadick, who sued the Calgary Stampede for wrongful dismissal after he was fired for excessive drinking, and who actually succeeded in convincing a judge that drinking was part of his job as Stampede promoter. And how could one fail to be engaged by the story of the two eccentric hillbilly King brothers from the Porcupine Hills, who chose to live like paupers on a ranch that was worth millions of dollars?

This is a book about people who dared to be different, characters who were either bad or good, naughty or nice, notorious or obscure, and who definitely would not tolerate being ignored. Some of the stories are cautionary tales about the dangers of alcohol. If booze had never touched their lives, Blackie Audett might not have become a bank robber, Emilio Picariello could not have become a bootlegger, Dorothy Joudrie might not have shot her husband, and D'arcy Scott might have enjoyed a long career in radio. Some are stories about public performers, inveterate attention-seekers, politicians, and entertainers who lived by the Oscar Wilde maxim that the only thing worse than being talked about is not being talked about. Some are stories about the very strange folks who put the lie to the notion that Britain is the only place in the world where people are allowed to talk to trees and put lemonade in their beer.

My sources, for the most part, are secondhand. I have acknowledged the principal books I consulted at the back of this volume. I also owe a debt to the dozens of mostly uncredited newspaper and magazine writers who provided me with additional raw material through their clippings. Journalism, they say, is history on the run, and I am grateful to the many sprinters and middle-distance runners who reached the finish line before I came trailing along behind. I don't believe in footnotes, but if I did, every page would contain a dozen of them. Wherever I found discrepancies in the available information, I tried as best I could to reconcile the differences and to produce the most credible version of the story. As the author, I take full responsibility for any errors that may have resulted.

My thanks to Charlene Dobmeier, publisher of Fifth House Ltd., for suggesting this project. I also want to thank Allan Shute of Edmonton's Tree Frog Press for all the time he spent in the City of Edmonton Archives and for all the photocopying and faxing he did on my behalf. He contributed more time and ideas than is evident from the text. In Calgary I remain constantly grateful for the resources of the Glenbow Museum and the Calgary Public Library, without which I could never do this work. Plus, I want to thank the many people, too numerous to mention here, who suggested candidates for this book. I had a lot of fun researching and writing it. I hope you have fun reading it.

Brian Brennan
Calgary, June 2002

John "One Pound One" Rowand

Hudson's Bay Company factor

1789–1854

John Rowand became the brawling, roaring, fur-trade king of the Prairies when two companies—the giant Hudson's Bay Company and the upstart North West Company—controlled the trade in what was then Rupert's Land. His bullying methods and fierce temper, combined with his love of horses and outdoor adventure, defined him as a certain kind of Albertan long before the province was founded. In fact, Ralph Klein seemed to have inherited, 150 years later, both Rowand's forceful leadership skills and his scrappy personality.

The son of an Irish physician, Rowand grew up in Montreal when it was the bustling headquarters of the fur trade. As a child, he dreamed of joining those intrepid voyageurs who journeyed across the continent by canoe to barter with the Natives for furs. At age fourteen, he joined the North West Company as an apprentice clerk and accepted a posting at Fort Augustus, a fortified trading post on the banks of the North Saskatchewan River near where Edmonton's Rossdale power plant stands today. From there he became part of the movement to push the trade across the Rocky Mountains to the Pacific.

In 1810, at age twenty-one, Rowand married Louise Umfrieville, a Métis who lived in a tipi outside the Fort Augustus stockade. She was a single mother, five years Rowand's senior, with what one historian has described as "several children by one or more absconding fur-trade fathers." She turned out to be the only person ever capable of putting the belligerent Rowand in his place.

The bare-bones historical account of Rowand's betrothal to Umfrieville, as chronicled by J.G. MacGregor in his book, *John Rowand, Czar of the Prairies*, says she found him lying in agony on the ground with a broken leg after being thrown from his horse during a hunting trip. She set his leg and nursed him back to health, and he showed his gratitude by marrying her. That was the beginning and the end of the story until writer Fred Stenson, in his novel *The Trade*, imaginatively put a contemporary feminist spin on the tale. According to Stenson, the "truth" of the story is that Umfrieville sat on her cart for hours, staring at Rowand in silence while he writhed on the ground.

Her silence spoke volumes, wrote Stenson. She was letting Rowand know that he was in her power and that he would become supper for the wolves if she decided to abandon him. On the other hand, if she were to fix his leg and save his life, he would have to meet certain conditions: He would have to be better behaved than some of the other traders she had known; he would have to undertake not to beat her or their children; and he could not force her to work more than was reasonable and fair. When Rowand tacitly agreed to these conditions, Umfrieville fixed his leg, hauled him onto her cart, and brought him back to the safety of the fort. Rowand, to his credit, kept his end of the bargain. To the end of his life, he had a limp to remind him of it. His employees used the onomatopoeic term "One Pound One"—i.e., one pound plus one shilling in English currency—to describe his halting gait.

Rowand lived and worked at Fort Augustus until 1815, when his bosses asked him to bring sword and musket to the Red River Settlement in what is now Manitoba. The ongoing struggles between the North West Company and the rival Hudson's Bay Company had escalated into armed hostilities, and Rowand—who was by now a squat, heavyset man weighing about three hundred pounds—had volunteered to fight for the cause. After a series of minor skirmishes at Red River, the war erupted into the bloody Battle of Seven Oaks in June 1816, when the Northwesters and their Métis allies killed the Bay's local governor, Robert Semple, and twenty of his men. A series of retaliatory strikes and lawsuits followed, after which, in 1821, the two companies agreed to settle their differences by amalgamating under the banner of the Hudson's Bay Company.

By 1823, Rowand's reputation as a tough, fearless, no-nonsense trader was such that the Hudson's Bay Company appointed him

Hudson's Bay Company factor John Rowand: "Any man
who is not dead after three days' sickness is not sick at all."
(GLENBOW ARCHIVES NA-1747-1)

chief factor—in effect, general manager—for its vast fur-trading region, which covered the present provinces of Alberta and Saskatchewan. "Big Mountain," as the Natives dubbed Rowand, lived at Edmonton House, a fort that the Hudson's Bay's autocratic governor, Sir George Simpson, described as "the most troublesome post in the Indian country." Located within the same stockade as the old Fort Augustus post, Edmonton House quickly grew under Rowand's control into a pivotal fort. As well as being an efficient and profitable outpost for the company, it was also a key transportation and communication hub on the trans-Canada trading route between Lake Winnipeg and Fort Vancouver.

Rowand spoke English, French, Cree, and Blackfoot, all essential languages in the fur trade. He also knew how to use his fists—another essential attribute. He told people that he believed only in God and the company and, if he had to choose between the two, God would lose. Nonetheless, he was an effective leader. Through bullying and threatening, he kept competing Native bands from warring with one another, and kept his grumbling employees from fomenting rebellion.

Though his limp slowed him down, Rowand worked as hard or harder than his men, and he refused to accept illness as an excuse for their slacking off. "Any man who is not dead after three days' sickness is not sick at all," he boomed. When the employees complained to Simpson about Rowand's cruelty, the governor defended the burly factor by explaining that he was "of a fiery disposition and bold as a lion."

In 1829, one of the North Saskatchewan River's frequent floods hit Edmonton House, and that gave Rowand an excuse to rebuild the fort on higher ground immediately below where the provincial legislature stands today. As befitted his stature as the fur trade's big boss for all the western Prairies, he built the biggest mansion between Winnipeg and the Rocky Mountains. The local Natives called it "Big House." Others called it "Rowand's Folly." It measured one hundred feet long by thirty feet wide, stood four levels tall with verandahs around every storey, and boasted the region's first glass windows, shipped from England in barrels of molasses to prevent breakage. The main dining hall could seat 150, and the grand ballroom doubled during the springtime as a storage room for fur bales. On the grounds nearby, Rowand kept a large dairy farm and bred racehorses, testing their speed and endurance on his two-mile racetrack.

During the 1830s, Rowand faced growing trade competition from the Americans, who were sending their steamboats up the Missouri River to the Milk River and beyond. These boats provided them with the means to supply trade goods cheaply, carry furs quickly, and deal with the heavy buffalo robes that the Bay couldn't handle. Responding to the American threat, Rowand sent his men to set up Peigan Post on the Bow River near present-day Morley. But the Peigan refused to switch allegiance back to the Bay, and the post closed within two years. Rowand had better success when he set up the post of Fort Pitt, just east of the modern Alberta-Saskatchewan border.

Rowand lived and worked at the Big House for more than twenty years and witnessed several changes in prairie life during that time. These included the decline of the buffalo herd, the emergence of cattle drives, the destructive impact of inter-tribal wars, liquor, starvation, and disease on the Blackfoot and the Cree, and the arrival of the Christian missionaries. Rowand initially hoped that these missionaries would relieve the Hudson's Bay Company of the responsibility of caring for the destitute Natives and encourage them to be a cheap and docile labour force for the fur trade. But he soon clashed with Methodist missionary Robert Rundle, who did not want the Natives working on a Sunday. "The worst thing for the trade is these ministers and priests," bellowed Rowand. "The Natives will never work half so well now—they like praying and singing. The Indians will soon forget to hunt. The fort is not a place to keep ministers."

Rowand remained at Fort Edmonton until 1854, when he decided to retire to Montreal. He had considered retiring twenty years earlier, but told himself then that he was too poor to quit. In 1854 he was sixty-five, his wife had been dead for five years, his seven children had grown to adulthood, and he felt it was time for him to move on. But he only made it as far as Fort Pitt, where his son John was chief trader. Rowand died of a heart attack while trying to break up a fist fight between two of his son's boatmen.

He left a sizable estate, valued at thirty thousand pounds, which went to his three unmarried daughters. He also left a stable of two hundred horses, half of which remained in his estate while the other half reverted to the Hudson's Bay Company.

Few mourned his passing. One man said it was his happiest day to see the scoundrelly old trader dead. Rowand had asked to be buried in Montreal, and so his boss, Simpson, made arrangements the following spring to exhume the body and move it. But it wasn't so easy in those days to transport a body halfway across the country. To resolve the problem, Simpson decided on a gruesome solution. He ordered a Native woman to boil the flesh from the bones to reduce the weight. The story goes that loud curses were heard as the pot boiled. Even after six months in the ground, there was enough fat rendered from the remains to make a sizable batch of soap.

The Natives sealed Rowand's bones in a keg with rum added as a preservative and put the remains in a canoe for transportation to Hudson Bay. But when a storm hit Lake Winnipeg, the frightened voyageurs threw the barrel overboard, believing it to be cursed. It bounced around in the water for several days, until eventually it was retrieved and continued on its journey to York Factory on Hudson Bay. Ships from York Factory sailed only to England, so the keg carried on to London and then to Liverpool, where it sat in a storage shed for years until someone finally realized it was actually meant to go to Montreal. Four years after he died in a fist fight, John Rowand, reduced from man-mountain to a keg of bones, arrived at his final resting place beneath a grand memorial in Montreal's Mount Royal Cemetery.

Postscript

In 1896, the newly formed Edmonton Golf and Country Club acquired Rowand's mansion at Fort Edmonton for use as a clubhouse. The members laid out a five-hole course on what are now the grounds of the provincial legislature, and revived the name "Rowand's Folly" for the clubhouse. Somehow that seemed the right name to give to a place where golfers commiserate about missed putts and hooked drives. The old mansion served as a watering hole for the golfers until 1906, when there was an outbreak of smallpox in Edmonton. The city appropriated the building for use as an isolation hospital—a "pest house," they called it—and when the outbreak was over, the city burned the place down. A replica of the Rowand mansion was later installed in Edmonton's Fort Edmonton Historic Park, on the banks of the North Saskatchewan River, three miles upstream from the original location.

Henry "Twelve-Foot" Davis

Peace River trader

1820–1900

~

James "Peace River Jim" Cornwall

Peace River promoter

1869–1955

Twelve-Foot Davis and Peace River Jim Cornwall were the Dr. Jekyll and Mr. Hyde of the mighty Peace River country of northwestern Alberta, a broad frontier that has always attracted a goodly share of larger-than-life characters. Though different in terms of temperament and personality—Davis was quiet and generous, Cornwall was loud and self-serving—and separated in age by almost half a century, they became close friends and synonymous with the region's reputation as a mecca for colourful pioneers.

Davis had already been in the region for close to thirty years when Cornwall arrived in 1898 to set up a trading post at Lesser Slave Lake, near where High Prairie stands today. Born in Vermont in 1820, Davis worked briefly as a pastry cook in Boston and was among the adventurers who crossed the continent by wagon in 1849 to search for gold in California. He then trekked northward to search for gold along the Upper Fraser River in the newly established British colony called British Columbia.

A short man, barely five feet tall, Davis acquired his "twelve-foot" nickname in 1864 after he arrived at the gold-rush town of Barkerville in the Cariboo Mountains. Though unable to read or write, he was savvy enough to notice that two of the richest mining

Blind "Twelve-Foot" Davis (on cart) en route to Edmonton with his furs.
"He was every man's friend and never locked his cabin door."
(GLENBOW ARCHIVES NA-4035-119)

claims along Williams Creek took up a total of 212 feet, when they were actually registered at only 100 feet apiece. That meant there had to be a twelve-foot gap between the two claims. Davis filed on that gap, extracted twenty thousand dollars in gold from the narrow claim, and became known thereafter as Twelve-Foot Davis. The ultimate stamp of approval for a miner, he discovered, was to receive a nickname from his fellow prospectors.

Davis converted his gold into trading goods and set up a chain of small trading posts along the Peace River. He bought his supplies in Quesnel, British Columbia, and took them upstream by canoe along the Fraser and Parsnip Rivers to what is now Williston Lake. He then travelled eastward along the Peace to Fort Dunvegan, where he set up his main trading post across the river from the big Hudson's Bay Company post. On average, the river journey from Quesnel to Dunvegan took Davis about two months. It took longer if he decided to stay at one of the posts he built along the way. These were small storage cabins that Davis kept stocked with food and blankets and always left open. If hungry travellers needed food, they simply helped themselves and settled their accounts later. Because of this, Davis built a reputation as a trusting and generous man.

Though he never kept books or records, Davis always knew what he owed and never failed to settle his debts. A popular story circulating in the Peace recalls the time a northern trapper turned over a season's worth of beaver skins to Davis and died before receiving payment. Ten years later, the trapper's son came to trade. "Before your father died, he left some beaver skins with me," said Davis. "I'll pay you now."

During the 1880s, Davis began to acquire his supplies from Edmonton rather than Quesnel. He adjusted his trading routes to conduct his bartering business northward along the Peace, from what is now the town of Peace River to Fort Vermilion. He became famous for his hospitality, his extraordinary pumpkin pies—which he had learned to make during his early years as a pastry cook—and for his ability, despite his small size, to pack two-hundred-pound loads over portages. The local Natives dubbed him "the Wolf" because of his feats of strength and endurance.

By 1898, when Peace River Jim came to the region, Davis had

made hundreds of friends among the whites, Natives, and immigrant Chinese he employed as freight packers and canoeists. Asked to explain how he remained friends with so many of them, Davis replied, "Maybe it's because they all need smiles and all need grub, and I keep a good stock of both. So I just smile at them and feed them."

Peace River Jim became one of those friends after he settled in the Peace at age twenty-nine (Davis was then seventy-eight), fresh from making a small fortune as a riverboat pilot ferrying Klondike gold seekers through the rapids near Athabasca Landing. Born in Brantford, Ontario, Cornwall gained his boating experience starting as a teenager, when he shipped aboard sailing vessels on the Great Lakes, and in later years, when he sailed before the mast on the North Atlantic. Lured north by the Yukon gold rush, he decided he could make more money piloting prospectors through the Athabasca rapids at twenty-five dollars per passenger than he could panning for gold.

After trying his luck briefly as a farmer, Cornwall opened a string of trading posts throughout the Peace River region in partnership with a fur trader named Fletcher Bredin. They set a precedent by becoming the first traders to use cash instead of beaver skins as the medium of exchange in Canada's North. Cornwall achieved another first when he became the federal government's official mail carrier for the North. By his own account, he wrested the contract away from the Hudson's Bay Company (which considered mail for the North its own private domain). He then proceeded to carry the mail on his back from Edmonton to Peace River, a distance of four hundred miles, for one dollar per envelope. Later, he carried the mail by dogsled and claimed he could "out-run any man in the world behind a team of dogs."

His claims are all part of the Cornwall mythology. He also told people that he was a gunrunner in Venezuela during his early twenties, that he shot bears for a living when he first moved north, and that he discovered oil at Fort Norman in the Northwest Territories. Asked why he never capitalized on his oil strike, Cornwall replied that when he approached Imperial Oil about drilling, they refused. Too far, they said.

"Peace River Jim" Cornwall carrying mail to Northern Alberta:
"I could out-run any man in the world behind a team of dogs."
(GLENBOW ARCHIVES NA-2760-8)

Twelve-Foot Davis was nearing the end of his life, blind and lame, when Cornwall brought his tall tales and his trading activities to the Peace. The story goes that the two men were sitting one day on a hilltop overlooking the scenic location where the Peace and Smoky Rivers merge into one big waterway. "When the time comes," said Davis, "this is where I want to be buried." Cornwall assured him that his wish would be fulfilled. But it would be a while before Cornwall was able to deliver on his promise.

Davis spent his last year in an Anglican mission at what was then called Lesser Slave Lake, now known as Grouard. Asked by a nursing sister if he was afraid to die, Davis replied, "No, miss, why should I be afraid? I never killed anybody, I never stole from anybody, and I always kept open-house for all travellers all my life. No, miss, I'm not afraid to die." He died on September 13, 1900, at age eighty, and was buried at the Anglican mission.

Cornwall, busy elsewhere with his various trading and other activities, was unaware of his friend's death. In 1903, he and Bredin sold their trading posts to Revillon Frères, a Paris-based company. Cornwall took the money and set up the Northern Transportation Company to operate paddlewheel steamboats on the Athabasca and Slave Rivers and on Lesser Slave Lake. During his years as a trader, Cornwall had come to recognize the agricultural and resource-development opportunities in the Peace River area, but he knew that an efficient north-south transportation link was needed to make large-scale settlement possible. His boats were an important part of that link, but they were limited to operating in spring and summer and were isolated by the barriers to navigation that existed along the Athabasca. The Peace River area was additionally isolated by a lack of roads and railways through the hundreds of miles of wilderness and muskeg that separated it from the more settled areas to the south.

In 1905, Cornwall formed the Athabasca Railway Company, and for three years he tried unsuccessfully to raise funds for a rail link from Edmonton to his sailing docks at Athabasca Landing. He sold his interests in 1908 to the eastern syndicate that created the Alberta and Great Waterways Railway, a company implicated in Alberta's first big political scandal. Alberta premier Alexander Rutherford, appointed when the province was founded in 1905, was accused along with his Liberal colleagues of accepting kickbacks from the New York financial firm that insured the railway bonds. The scandal forced Rutherford and several of his cabinet ministers to resign, though a judicial inquiry later cleared the premier of any personal involvement. It is not known whether Cornwall, who became Liberal member of the legislative assembly for Peace River in 1908, was directly involved in the scandal.

As MLA, Cornwall became a powerful voice for the North, lobbying tirelessly for telegraph lines and railways. He saw some results in 1909, when the Canadian Northern received permission to build a rail line north from Edmonton to Athabasca Landing, along the route of an old wagon trail. Cornwall decided that this might be the link needed to open up the Peace and thus attract settlers from the United States and eastern Canada. He asked the Edmonton Board of Trade to help him promote such settlement, but it refused to have anything to do with the scheme.

Undeterred, Cornwall decided to promote the area himself, using his own money to organize a four-week tour of the region for eighteen journalists, agriculturalists, and businessmen from Canada and the United States. The 1910 expedition received extensive coverage in magazines and newspapers and paved the way for future media publicity about the Peace, much of it generated by Cornwall himself. "The North is coming into its own," he said in a typical speech. "It's a young man's country, a big empire, and surely will prove the salvation of Alberta because it contains perhaps the greatest extent of virgin mineral country in the world."

Cornwall served as MLA for just four years, quitting politics in 1912 to concentrate on his transportation and navigation interests. But his favoured route into the Peace through Athabasca Landing and west across Lesser Slave Lake lost its popularity when the Grand Trunk Pacific and the Canadian Northern pushed their rail lines westward from Edmonton and provided a new and easier route into the Peace. The town of Edson became the jumping-off point for a wilderness trail—later an improved highway—to what is now Grande Prairie. By 1916, the Athabasca Landing route was no longer being used, and Cornwall, at age forty-seven, was off serving his country in the First World War.

When he returned from overseas, after commanding the 218th Battalion Irish Guards—a unit formed to build railways behind Allied lines in France—Peace River Jim was Lieutenant-Colonel J.K. Cornwall, decorated for bravery with the *Croix de Guerre* from France and the Distinguished Service Order from King George V at Buckingham Palace. He resumed his trading and transportation activities and continued to promote the Peace, loudly upsetting staid boardroom meetings from Montreal to Vancouver as he bellowed about the tremendous commercial possibilities in the North.

He was frequently in the news, featured in stories where he made glowing comments about the North and disparaging remarks about almost everyplace else. The East, he boomed, was "full of cranks, fakers, and political stuffed shirts." Toronto was "the most snobbish, stuffy city in the land." Not even Edmonton escaped his wrath. "The merchants of Edmonton are pariahs," he said. "They accept all the business from the North and they give nothing in return." This was a reference to the fact that northern mining prospectors often had difficulty obtaining loans in Edmonton. The only Edmonton businessman for whom he had consistently kind words was a pawnshop owner named Pete Glassman. "When you want credit from another Edmonton merchant, he wants your whole arm as security," Cornwall declared. "Pete Glassman never asks you for more than two fingers."

When the era of the bush pilot arrived in Canada's North during the 1920s, Cornwall abandoned his shipping interests and trading posts and began roaming across the northland in search of minerals. Based in what is now Fort McMurray, he dabbled in the oil business in the Northwest Territories and invested in uranium mining in northern Saskatchewan. "Somebody has to go ahead," he said about his various groundbreaking initiatives. "If you make money while doing it, fine. If not, it does not matter. There's enough thrill in blazing a new trail." At the same time as he opened up new opportunities for himself, Cornwall carried the message of Canada's North throughout the world. He actively promoted the region in cities from London to Hong Kong and also spoke out about the lack of medical treatment available for Natives in remote areas. "The way we have treated our Indians is a national crime," he said in a 1934 speech in

London. "The condition of the Indians is a disgrace to a civilized country."

Sometimes his public pronouncements revealed a cleverly roguish sense of humour. During the rise of William Aberhart's Social Credit party in 1935, Cornwall dismissed the party's economic theories as nothing more than sleight of hand. "You can't make rabbit stew with rabbits you just pull out of a hat," he declared. "You have to have real rabbits, not trick ones." He predicted that the people of the North would never swallow the "synthetic meal" being served up by the Social Crediters.

Cornwall continued to preach the gospel of the North until he was in his eighties. He died at age eighty-six, in November 1955, at the Colonel Belcher hospital in Calgary. Newspapers across Canada hailed him as the North's most effective ambassador. *The Calgary Herald*, in a reverential editorial, said Cornwall did more to show the world the country north of Edmonton "than any government, church or individual." *The Montreal Star*, adopting a tone more suited to the man's colourful personality, described him as a "husky, cheerful, hard-muscled vagabond." The editorial concluded: "How Peace River Jim hewed for himself a place in the frozen wilderness, and how he became the virtual dictator of its sentiments by sheer force of personality—these are the commonplaces about Jim Cornwall."

As for Cornwall's promise to Twelve-Foot Davis, he did in fact make arrangements to have his old friend buried on the hillside a thousand feet above the town of Peace River, many years after Twelve-Foot's death. Cornwall received permission to have the body exhumed from the grave at Lesser Slave Lake, lashed the coffin to a toboggan, journeyed the one hundred miles to Peace River, and buried it on the hill with one of the most spectacular views in the region. On the gravestone, shaped to resemble a poplar stump, he inscribed an epitaph for Davis that included the words: "He was every man's friend, and never locked his cabin door."

Postscript

The Twelve-Foot Davis gravestone became a popular Alberta tourist attraction, drawing thousands of visitors annually. It also became a hangout for vandals and for late-night drinkers. Eventually, there wasn't much left of Peace River Jim's tribute to his old friend. Vandals smashed up much of it and spray-painted the rest. The town of Peace River responded by replacing the damaged gravestone with a concrete mausoleum containing some of the original granite and an interpretive sign that included the original epitaph. It's a closed prison for all eternity for the man who never locked a door in life.

Thomas "Gunner Jingo" Strange

Army officer

1831–1925

Although the 1885 North-West Rebellion took place mainly in what is now Saskatchewan, there is an important Alberta aspect to the story of this armed confrontation between Canadian government forces and dispossessed Natives and Métis. It rarely rates more than a few paragraphs in the published histories of the period because it involved deterrence more than armed conflict. Yet it highlights the effective role that the eccentric Major-General Thomas Bland Strange played in the rebellion. The retired British army officer took charge of the defence of the Alberta district at a time when news of insurgent victories in Saskatchewan were reverberating across the Prairies and causing nervous white settlers to bar their doors and seek refuge in fortified police posts.

Strange had retired to a ranch east of Calgary when he answered the call to defend the interests of his adopted home in the Canadian West. Born in India into a Scottish military family that traced its soldiering roots back to the Normans, Strange saw action as an artillery officer in the Indian Mutiny of 1857, when Bengal soldiers rebelled against British rule in India, and he received four citations for bravery along with many lessons in the madness of war. In his autobiography, which he titled *Gunner Jingo's Jubilee*, he wrote of killing enemy soldiers with his sword and of comrades who were "drunk with blood and plunder and thirsty for vengeance." He adopted the nickname "Gunner Jingo" to express his chauvinistic patriotism and support for an aggressive foreign policy.

After seven bloody years in India, followed by six more peaceful years in England, Strange was posted to Canada in 1871. Britain had withdrawn its garrisons, and Strange was one of two British officers sent to take charge of the first military schools organized by the

Cree chief Big Bear and General T. Bland Strange, as depicted in the *Illustrated War News*, 1885. "On the conduct of yourselves and your bands, your future treatment will depend." (GLENBOW ARCHIVES NA-1353-16)

young Canadian nation. He was based in Quebec City, where he told people he was "commandant of the citadel."

Strange spent ten years in Quebec, laying the groundwork for the development of the Canadian artillery and often living up to his reputation as a warrior. When a mob staged a riot outside the Quebec parliament buildings in 1873 to protest the transfer of a humanist's body from a Protestant to a Catholic cemetery, Strange ordered his soldiers to draw their bayonets and drive the rioters away. Afterwards he boasted that his men had shot down "half a dozen men and a cab horse" and left the leader of the rioters "lying in the gutter in a pool of blood."

Considered too controversial and eccentric for more senior command, Strange was forcibly retired from the British imperial army in 1881 at age fifty. He complained in a letter to his superiors that a man of his age was "considered too old to lead one hundred men, but an octogenarian is not too old to run or ruin an Empire." Unwilling to settle for a sedentary life, he launched a second career as a rancher at Gleichen, Alberta, adjoining the Blackfoot reserve, sixty miles east of Calgary. With capital raised from shareholders in eastern Canada and India, he leased a spread of seventy thousand acres and stocked it with three stallions, one hundred mares, and a few hundred cattle. By 1884, he was able to report to the *Calgary Herald* that he had seven hundred cattle and three hundred horses grazing on his range.

Strange built his ranch headquarters next to the Bow River, which he used as a frozen highway to Calgary in winter and for transporting logs in summer. The house, which he named Strangmuir, was a two-storey structure, large enough to accommodate Strange and his wife, their two sons, three daughters, an Irish cook, and a female cousin. Among its features was an elegant English tea room with a piano. But that's not to suggest Strange lived the life of the indolent upper-class Englishman. In fact, he worked as hard as any of his young ranch hands, cutting timber and breaking horses.

Strange had a testy relationship with his Blackfoot neighbours, whom he suspected of stealing his livestock. He accused them of chasing away horses "with the view of getting rewards for bringing them back." He also had harsh words for the local judiciary, which he accused of treating accused horse thieves too leniently and frequently recording cop-out verdicts of "not guilty, but don't do it again." Nothing was to be gained by such hypocrisy on the part of the authorities, said Strange. The Natives had "no tangible grounds of complaint beyond their natural dislike to seeing white men occupy their country."

On March 26, 1885, the first shots of the North-West Rebellion were fired, at the tiny hamlet of Duck Lake north of today's Rosthern in what is now Saskatchewan. A skirmish between an advancing column of mounted policemen and citizen volunteers and a large force of Métis and Natives left twelve police and volunteers dead, and also resulted in the deaths of six Métis and Natives. Three days later, on March 29, Strange received a telegram from Adolphe Caron, Canada's minister of militia and defence: "Can you get a corps? Would like to see you at the front again." Strange wired back to say he would be happy to organize a home guard for the protection of local ranching interests. Instead, he found himself commanding, as he proudly reported, "a country larger than England and Wales."

It took about three weeks for Strange to raise what came to be known as the Alberta Field Force. During this time, the hostilities in Saskatchewan included skirmishes and looting of trading posts at Battleford, Lac La Biche, Saddle Lake, and other settlements. At Frog Lake, north of present-day Lloydminster, a deadly confrontation by the warriors of Big Bear's Plains Cree band killed nine white men, including two priests. Strange and his troops worked first to calm the panic-stricken residents of Calgary and Edmonton, who were living next to large reserves, and then marched northeast to capture the perpetrators of the Frog Lake massacre.

Strange's seven-hundred-member ragtag battalion of cowboys, ranchers, Mounties, scouts, and newly enlisted soldiers from Winnipeg, Montreal, and Quebec City played only a secondary role in the military campaign. The main action was at Batoche, northeast of present-day Saskatoon, where Métis leader Louis Riel had established his rebel stronghold and where General Frederick Middleton, chief commander of the Canadian militia, directed the opposing government forces. A third government column, under Colonel William Otter, was assigned to relieve the fort at Battleford, which was besieged by a Cree band under Poundmaker, the adopted son of the Blackfoot chief Crowfoot.

Ottawa began to have second thoughts about Strange's appointment almost from the time he took charge of military operations in the Alberta district. His superior officer, General Middleton, viewed Strange as a dangerous "crank," and Strange's increasingly autocratic behaviour toward Natives who had not joined the rebellion prompted Middleton and the militia minister Caron to try and relieve Strange of his command. However, because Strange was on the march, he was beyond their communications reach.

Strange and his troops met no opposition as they travelled from Calgary to Edmonton assuring nervous settlers that the government was defending their interests and warning local Natives that "on the conduct of yourselves and your bands, your future treatment will depend." During seventy days of campaigning, the only battles the Alberta Field Force fought were a couple of minor skirmishes with the Frog Lake Cree and a final rescue operation when they effected the release of forty hostages held by Big Bear's band. Big Bear was subsequently convicted of treason and sentenced to three years in prison. Released after two years due to failing health, he returned to the Little Pine Reserve in Saskatchewan to find his wife gone and his band scattered. With nowhere else to go, Big Bear remained on the reserve where, broken in health and spirit, he died at age sixty on January 17, 1888.

Strange received no official credit for his efforts as commander of the Alberta Field Force. His cleanup efforts at Frog Lake were overshadowed by the final defeat of the rebels at Batoche and by Riel's surrender on May 15, 1885. Although Strange had effectively prevented the Natives in the Alberta district from joining the rebellion, his role was downplayed in General Middleton's official report to the government.

Little went right for Strange after that. He lost his British military pension because he had returned to active service during the rebellion, and Ottawa rejected him as a candidate for North-West Mounted Police commissioner. "He is too old altogether and too much of a mere gunner to have control of the police force," wrote Prime Minister John A. Macdonald, adding that Strange's "crazy" dislike of Natives amounted almost to "semi-insanity." Strange then attempted to enter federal politics as an independent member of parliament, but withdrew from the campaign after a few weeks, citing a lack of money.

In late 1887, Strange ended his ranching career. Economic reverses, ongoing problems with the local Natives, poor weather conditions, and an injury from a horse kick had dampened his optimism. He returned to England, saying "I have given the best years of my life to the service of Canada and I only want to get out of it and never see it more."

He lived in a London suburb for the rest of his life. He published his autobiography in 1894 and died in 1925 at age ninety-four, long forgotten in the province where he had raised and commanded his own fighting force. The *Calgary Herald* neglected to report his death. The *Albertan* did give it a brief mention but misspelled his nickname as Gunner "Jinga." Forty years previously, a writer had said of Strange, "The Dominion owes him a deep debt of gratitude." At the time of his death, he was virtually unknown, although the government did give his name to a mountain near Jasper. And a Calgary historian named Jack Dunn published a book, *The Alberta Field Force of 1885*, which provides a full account of the last time Albertans fought a war on Canadian soil. It tells a colourful tale of the crusty old gunner who readily answered the call when Canada asked for a military leader to help preserve its grand vision of a nation from sea to sea.

Isaac Barr

Colonist

1847–1937

History has not been kind to the Reverend Isaac Barr. In 1903, the Anglican clergyman from Ontario convinced two thousand British bank clerks, butchers, and ex-Boer War soldiers to abandon their urban lives and set up a farming paradise in the wilds of the Canadian West near what is now Lloydminster. But when things started to go wrong and harsh prairie realities replaced rosy dreams, Reverend Barr became the scapegoat. Some say he was inept, some say he was a crook. Author Helen Evans Reid, in a 1963 *Maclean's* magazine article, called him "the clerical con man who helped settle the West." But Reid subsequently did more research, recanted her original story, and published a book portraying Barr as an honest but misguided fool, more to be pitied than censured.

This much is known for sure: Barr promised the British emigrants more than he could ever deliver. He said the journey by ship, train, and wagon would be a "grand tour," luxurious and comfortable, with pleasant accommodations along the way. The winters in Canada would be bracing yet healthful, the land would be free, the growing seasons lush, and the farming would be bountiful. It all sounded appealing to Britons battered by depressed economic conditions in the wake of the Boer War. Only problem was, little of it turned out to be true.

Did Barr intentionally exaggerate or was he simply ill advised? His background suggests that he had a tendency to be unstable. He never spent more than one year at any given parish after he became a minister in 1871. In each instance, he had a disagreement with the congregation over the amount of money he should be paid and a disagreement with the bishop over the doctrinal purity of his sermons. Finally, in 1883, Barr left Canada under a cloud and fled to the

United States, where he continued to drift from parish to parish for the next nineteen years.

In 1902, he arrived in London with a vision. Inspired by Cecil Rhodes, the British imperialist and business magnate, Barr developed a grand plan for setting up a British agricultural colony on the Canadian Prairies. Americans were already taking advantage of the free land being offered by the Canadian government, and Barr thought that the British should be doing the same. A brief posting at Prince Albert in 1875 had convinced him that the region held great potential for immigrants.

Barr asked another Anglican clergyman, the Reverend George Lloyd, to help him with his plans for bringing the colonists over. Canadian immigration officials were unsure about supporting the scheme because they knew nothing about Barr aside from what he had told them about his experience with settlement in the United States. But Barr went ahead regardless, holding public meetings and signing up people by the hundreds. Soon the scheme was too far along to stop. When the two thousand emigrants left in the spring of 1903, they comprised the largest group of British subjects ever to depart for the Canadian northwest. Only twenty percent had any actual experience with agricultural work, and some of these stretched the definition to include milk delivery and gardening.

Things began to go wrong even before the emigrants left England. Barr had ordered three ships, but most of the passengers were crammed into a converted troop ship meant to hold only 550 people. "More like an excursion steamer to Clacton than an Atlantic liner," observed one emigrant. Instead of luxurious accommodations, the ship provided large dormitories with tiny bunks and hay-filled mattresses. Those who came without blankets had to sleep in their clothes.

The amount of luggage overwhelmed the ship's crew. Barr had told the colonists they should bring along sewing machines, feather beds, fine china, and a "good English saddle," and added that he would transport their musical instruments free of charge. Most chose to bring their pianos, as many as five hundred of them, according to one estimate.

Bad food contributed to the problems on board. "Some of the

eggs had chickens ready to hatch," said one colonist. When Barr met with the steerage passengers to discuss the problems, one of them threw a stale ship's biscuit that struck him in the mouth and knocked him down. "I'm through with you people," shouted Barr. "You're a lot of savages." He took refuge in his cabin for the rest of the voyage while his clergyman colleague, Reverend Lloyd, tried to deal with the passengers' concerns.

After eleven uncomfortable days, the colonists arrived at Saint John, New Brunswick, where their possessions were unceremoniously dumped in piles on the dock. Barr was accused of profiteering when, in preparation for the long train journey westward, he arranged to have eight thousand loaves of bread baked on board and sold to the colonists at ten cents a loaf. One colonist discovered after he left the ship that the same bread was available in Saint John at five cents a loaf.

The problems continued as the colonists journeyed westward. The coaches were crowded, noisy, and overheated, and food prices at the grocery stores en route were jacked up to extortion levels when merchants heard that a trainload of "wealthy" immigrants was passing through. Upon arrival at the end of the line at Saskatoon, the colonists discovered that nothing was ready for them. Most of their luggage had been left behind in Saint John and would not arrive for several weeks. Equipment and supplies needed for homesteading were also en route. The colonists lived in tents while waiting for their possessions to arrive, and many fell ill from drinking polluted water. The Saskatoon merchants took full advantage of the situation by inflating their prices. A story began circulating in the camp that Barr was receiving commissions from the merchants, which he first denied and then became defensive about. "If I have made money out of these supplies, I say it is none of your business," Barr said.

Two hundred of the colonists ran out of money while waiting in the camp in Saskatoon. They decided to abandon the idea of homesteading and instead accepted an offer from the Canadian government to find railway and surveying jobs for them. The rest of the colonists journeyed on to the tract of land that had been set aside for them, 160 miles to the west, on the line that now divides Alberta and Saskatchewan. By the time they arrived there, they were blaming

Barr for their every misfortune along the way. Hopelessly inept and unwilling to listen to the good advice of more seasoned settlers, they overloaded their wagons, became bogged down in the mud, and lost horses to injury and death. Some almost starved to death in a government camp that, due to negligence, failed to provide them with freshly baked bread and slaughtered beef. At a meeting in Battleford, halfway to their destination, the angry colonists demanded that Reverend Lloyd become their leader and forced Barr to sign over the money he had set aside for stores and medical supplies for the new colony.

Barr returned to England with plans for a new Canadian settlement scheme that never materialized. The colonists rejected their original plan to name their townsite Barrview (although they would continue to call themselves "Barr colonists") and instead named it Lloydminster after their new leader. Despite their initial stumbles, which led to their being ridiculed by other settlers as "green Englishmen," they adjusted quickly to the challenges of prairie life and proved to be quite industrious. Most built habitable sod houses on their homesteads, and by the fall of 1903 Lloydminster boasted a store, Anglican church, post office, telegraph office, drugstore, saddlery, and seventy-five houses. At Christmas, the colonists celebrated with a carol service, community dinner, and concert. Lloydminster would never again grow so quickly.

Lloyd left Lloydminster in 1905 and became bishop of Saskatchewan in 1922. Barr went to Australia and died in poverty after leading yet another failed settlement scheme. Arguments still persist about whether he was dishonest or simply incompetent.

Paddy Nolan

Lawyer

1862–1913

~

Caroline "Mother" Fulham

Pig keeper

1852–POST-1905

He was the clown prince of criminal defence lawyers, a wisecracking court jester who played to the gallery for laughs even when representing murderers and thieves. She was his first Canadian client, an illiterate keeper of pigs who settled disputes with her fists. They had little in common aside from the fact that both were Irish, yet they were drawn to one another like moths to a flame. For the courtroom spectators of frontier Calgary, Paddy Nolan and Caroline Fulham provided the best entertainment in town.

They arrived in Calgary at around the same time, toward the end of the 1880s. Nolan was a twenty-seven-year-old flour merchant's son from Limerick; Fulham was a Navy pensioner's wife from Dublin. Their first encounter came in April 1890, shortly after Nolan was admitted to the bar of the Northwest Territories, when he represented Fulham in an assault case. He had no hope of winning, or even of being paid, but he felt an obligation toward a fellow immigrant. "With Irish moss growing in her hair, and Irish belligerence in her fists, she must be Calgary's most notorious female citizen," he wrote admiringly in a letter to the folks back home.

Being Irish, for Nolan, was all that counted. He claimed to have been born on St. Patrick's Day, March 17, though he was in fact born

Lawyer Paddy Nolan. "A well of humour that never runs dry."
(GLENBOW ARCHIVES NA-452-3)

on March 3, and he viewed Calgary approvingly as his home away from home in the Canadian wilderness. "It's going to be bigger than Dublin some day," he confidently predicted when the permanent population of the frontier town was less than four thousand. "From what I've seen, I'd say a quarter of the population living here right now came from Ireland—or their parents came from Ireland—and about half of those who run the affairs of the town have Irish names." He suggested the name of the town should be changed to Little Dublin.

Nobody knows why Nolan decided to come to Calgary. He had achieved distinction as a law student in Ireland, winning the gold medal for oratory in a land of orators (though he did get kicked out of the Dublin University Philosophical Society for "persistent disorderly conduct at the society's meetings"). And he was a rising star of the Munster circuit in southern Ireland after being called to the Irish bar in 1885. After practising for four years, suddenly "in a moment of impulse I visited the steamship office, booked a passage, and paid the required twelve pounds for a ticket that would take me to Toronto by way of New York." A fellow traveller tried to persuade him to settle in New York rather than in a "Canadian village where they're still experimenting with civilization and not sure they want it." But Nolan wanted to see this wild-west place where he heard that Texas longhorns roamed the streets by day and "men figure they aren't decently dressed for work until they have their revolvers loaded and hanging on their belts."

Within a few months of his arrival, Nolan became the ninth lawyer to be registered in the Territories and the junior law partner of an Irish immigrant named T.B. Lafferty. "Mother" Fulham, as he called her, was one of Lafferty's regular clients, and he was happy to pass her on to the younger lawyer because he regarded her as a colossal nuisance. Nolan did not object. He could recognize good entertainment value when he saw it, and Fulham was the ideal character for his kind of courtroom comic opera.

Fulham was already well known to Calgary law enforcement authorities when Nolan took her on as a client. She lived downtown, kept pigs and a cow in her backyard, drank with the men at the Alberta Hotel, and often clashed with the police, who needed three

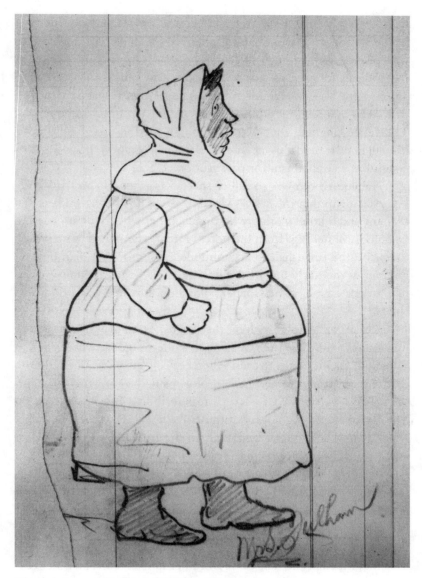

The only known likeness of "Mother" Fulham, sketched
by R. Randolph Bruce: "What made you think my cow could read?"
(GLENBOW ARCHIVES NA-2240-4)

men to subdue her whenever she became drunk and disorderly—which was often. Her husband, Jack, lived on a ranch in the foothills west of town and, though she could not read or write, she winked at the judge and gave as her occupation, "my husband's secretary." There were also two children, one a rebellious teenaged daughter who lived at a neighbour's house and defied all efforts to be tamed. The police laughed when Mother Fulham tried to rein the girl in by having her arrested on vagrancy charges. "Vagrancy" in police language was a euphemism for prostitution.

The courtroom was so full of spectators when Nolan first represented Fulham that the case—which involved an altercation between Fulham and a hotel worker who punched her when Fulham tried to take slops for her pigs from the hotel's garbage can—had to be moved to the nearby town hall to accommodate the crowd. Nolan did not disappoint them, though he did lose the case. "Even the stairway was full," reported a local newspaper. "For an hour there was a first-class circus."

While Nolan usually drew the laughs, Fulham was often good for a few chuckles with her own knife-tongued wit. When a Canadian Pacific Railway train killed her cow after it wandered onto the tracks near her home, she had Nolan sue the company for damages. The CPR refused to accept responsibility, on grounds that a "No Trespassing" sign was prominently displayed near the scene. "You damn fools," screamed Fulham at the CPR lawyers. "What made you think my cow could read?"

Two other stories, now part of early Calgary folklore and perhaps apocryphal, show how Fulham became Calgary's unofficial town fool at a time when people needed some comic relief from the hardships of frontier life. One tells of the time she accused a policeman of ripping some hair from her head and, when the evidence was checked, had to admit that the hair came from her horse's tail. The other tells how a doctor noticed her limping one day and offered to examine her leg. When she rolled down her stocking, he exclaimed, "I'll bet a dollar there's not another leg in Calgary as dirty as that." She quickly accepted the wager, rolled down her other stocking, and took the man's dollar.

When Fulham eventually sold her property and moved to

Vancouver after her husband died in 1903, the police heaved a collective sigh of relief. But those with a sense of humour knew Calgary's loss. Fulham got married again, to a Vancouver con artist named Michael Lyon, but the marriage lasted less than a year. In 1905, she returned briefly to Calgary and announced, "The coast is no fit place for a decent body to live." After that, Mother Fulham headed off to parts unknown and was heard from no more.

As for Paddy Nolan, he continued to provide Calgarians with comic relief for another eight years after Fulham left town, until he died suddenly of a heart attack at age fifty. "All the best criminals go to Paddy Nolan," wrote his pal Bob Edwards, editor of the satirical *Eye Opener* newspaper, and there was certainly enough comedy material in Nolan's courtroom performances to keep the newspaper's columns filled for months on end. Edwards described Nolan as "a well of humour that never runs dry."

While his cases only rarely featured a comic-opera character like Mother Fulham to guarantee laughter, they always provided Nolan with an opportunity to reveal his cleverness and wit. His biographer, Grant MacEwan, said Nolan even managed to draw laughter when defending the notorious outlaw Ernest Cashel, who daringly escaped from police custody in Calgary while awaiting execution on a murder conviction. A murder trial is obviously no laughing matter, said MacEwan, but when the accused man is the first to laugh—as Cashel apparently did—then it seemed appropriate for Nolan to use humour to relieve tension and boost morale.

MacEwan wrote the Nolan biography, *He Left Them Laughing When He Said Goodbye*, after first profiling the Irish lawyer in his *Fifty Mighty Men* collection, and there is a generous selection of the Nolan wit and wisdom in each volume. A characteristic example:

Nolan's arch-rival Richard B. Bennett, an outstanding lawyer before he became prime minister, faced off against Nolan in a case where the Irishman defended a Canadian Pacific Railway worker charged with stealing from his employer. Bennett, as chief counsel for the CPR, presented the case for the prosecution. Accompanied by an articling student, he arrived at the courtroom weighed down with an armload of law books.

Bennett did an effective job as prosecutor. Whenever the judge asked him to cite precedents, he turned to his assistant. "Boy, bring me Phipson on evidence," he commanded. "Boy, fetch me Lewin on trusts." The judge was impressed. So was the jury.

Nolan rose to address the jury. He didn't have an assistant, and he didn't have an armload of books, but he did have a strategy. Turning to an imaginary junior, he snapped his fingers and barked, "Boy, bring me Bennett on bluff." Pandemonium ensued, said MacEwan. "The jury laughed for ten minutes." Nolan secured his acquittal.

Aside from being a popular courtroom performer, Nolan was also well liked as an after-dinner speaker, debating society orator, and as an amateur actor and singer, drawing favourable reviews for his performances in Gilbert and Sullivan operettas. He never knew his lines until the last day of rehearsals, but he always stole the show when the curtain went up. Plus, he was a popular newspaper columnist. He wrote for the *Calgary Herald* from 1904 to 1906 and was described by the editor, G.C. Porter, as "the best associate editor I ever had."

Nolan never returned to Ireland, nor does he seem to have seriously considered doing so. He took Calgary to his heart and never looked back. In 1892, he married the former Minnie Lee of Toronto—he told her jokingly that he intended to ask Mother Fulham to be her bridesmaid—and said that while the marriage was not made it heaven, it was made in Calgary and "that had to be the next best place." When he died in 1913, his pal Bob Edwards was uncharacteristically serious for a change. "In life he always left them laughing when he said goodbye," wrote Edwards. "In this last goodbye, tears take the place of laughter."

William Sherman

Show business impresario

1868–1934

In the second decade of the twentieth century, long before popular culture turned violent and entertainment stopped being "live," Calgary played host to some of the finest stage performers in the world, thanks to the promotional efforts of an impresario who came right out of Hollywood central casting. With his diamond rings, gold pocket watch, and diamond-encrusted cigar holder, William Bowen Sherman looked every inch the stereotypical showman, the kind of persuasive huckster who could cable Sarah Bernhardt or Dame Nellie Melba and convince them to star on his stage.

He was a builder who liked to build monuments to himself. A vaudevillian from Ohio, Sherman left home at age seventeen to join a circus and came to Canada in 1901 with an animal act consisting of an "educated" goat. He dispensed with the goat when he decided it would never make him a headliner and turned instead to building parks, using his name and other people's money. He opened Sherman Park in Hamilton, Ontario, in 1902, and built a four-thousand-seat vaudeville house on the grounds that he called Sherman Auditorium.

The Hamilton vaudeville house burned down in 1904, after which Sherman travelled west as actor-manager with the touring Sherman & Summer Stock Company. In Calgary, the troupe played for two weeks at the Lyric Theatre, a six-hundred-seat playhouse owned by Senator James Lougheed, the entrepreneurial lawyer, politician, and land speculator whose grandson Peter would become premier of Alberta in 1971. After the two-week run at the Lyric, Sherman decided to keep his troupe in Calgary, basing the company at an old opera house that he leased and renamed Sherman Opera House.

Sherman and Lougheed soon became business partners. Theirs was an unlikely pairing because, at that time, it would have been

Theatrical promoter William Sherman and Mrs. Sherman:
"I want coloured people to see my show."
(GLENBOW ARCHIVES NA-460-7)

unseemly for a good Methodist like Lougheed to be associated with someone in the theatre. Calgary's Methodist minister, Reverend F. Langford, said the theatre was bad because it allowed people to "quiet the voice of conscience and keep up their cheerfulness in sin." Plus, the two men had nothing in common in terms of either background or personality. Lougheed was refined, cultured, and sophisticated. Sherman was squat, crude, and boorish. But Lougheed the entrepreneur knew a good business opportunity when he saw one. He and Sherman made money on their first promotional venture together, which involved leasing a railway car so that a Chicago theatre company could tour western Canada with a black-and-white minstrel show called *The Hottest Coon in Dixie*. After that success, they agreed that Sherman should become resident manager at the Lyric. Lougheed kept his hands clean by remaining in the background and putting up the money while his flamboyant partner acted as the front man.

Between 1905 and 1910, Sherman used Lougheed's money to lease and buy theatres in various Alberta towns, using the profits from one to support the next venture. He also booked vaudeville entertainment into halls across western Canada. In Calgary, Sherman turned an old curling rink into a vaudeville theatre that he named Sherman's Garden, and he converted an ice-skating rink into a five-thousand-seat arena, Sherman's Rink, that became the city's principal venue for hockey, roller skating, concerts, political meetings, prize fights, charity balls, and horse shows. Then he leased Calgary's Lyceum Theatre, renamed it the Orpheum, and used it for light musical comedy. And with the nucleus of his troupe at the Lyric, he formed the Sherman Great Northwest Circuit, touring his players to thirty-six theatres from Winnipeg to Vancouver. In Edmonton, meanwhile, Sherman leased both the Empire Theatre and the Edmonton Opera House, while in Lethbridge he leased the New Majestic Theatre.

Sherman and Lougheed launched their biggest theatrical venture in 1912 when they opened the palatial, $250,000, 1,504-seat Sherman Grand Theatre in downtown Calgary. "One of the finest and most commodious theatres in all of western Canada," said the English actor Johnston Forbes Robertson, who starred in the opening production of *The Passing of the Third Floor Back*, a melodrama adapted from a short story by Jerome K. Jerome. Sherman had wanted to build two theatres on the site, for an estimated $450,000, but Lougheed convinced him to scrap the second theatre and instead develop a six-storey commercial building on the block with just one theatre contained within.

While the interior of the Sherman Grand was tastefully decorated, with ornate woodwork and velvet curtains, there was one dissonant note in the harmony of the décor: a cheap fire curtain with crudely painted advertisements that clashed with the elegant proscenium. The first-night patrons denounced it as a horrible monstrosity. "If the theatre was a cheap vaudeville house, it would not matter," commented the *Calgary Herald*, adding that while Sherman did have to find a way to pay his bills, the garish fire curtain was not the answer. The Calgary *Albertan* commented that "a very passable theatre could have been constructed with the same seating capacity for little more than half the cost of the present building, and been far more profitable."

The criticism touched a sore spot. Sherman appeared onstage the next night to defend his curtain. Dressed in an ill-fitting tuxedo and mopping perspiration from his brow with a labourer's red handkerchief, he stood in front of the curtain and asked the audience what they thought of it. They responded by bursting into laughter. "Had he deliberately planned the routine, he could never have written a more effective comedy script," wrote historian Andrew King. The *Albertan* suggested that Sherman retire the curtain "and come out between acts and give the advertising orally."

Sherman didn't retire the curtain because it generated five hundred dollars a week. He also kept his ledger on the plus side by paying his backstage crew little and discharging them before the evening's performance was over. This prompted one opera company manager to complain in a letter to Senator Lougheed, "Sherman is a little too cheap. I had to hire extra men to get my stuff out of the house, because his crew of cheap stagehands had disappeared. Altogether, this engagement was very poor satisfaction from a man who pretends to run a theatre on theatre lines." It is not known what Lougheed said in reply.

Some of the biggest acts in early twentieth-century show business appeared on the Sherman Grand stage while Sherman was at the helm. They included Dame Nellie Melba, Margaret Anglin, John

Martin-Harvey, George Arliss, Sophie Tucker, and the scandal-tinged English actress Lillie Langtry, who was publicly known to have had a relationship with King Edward VII when he was Prince of Wales. Sherman also had an eye for talent on the way up. In September 1912, when a cowboy showman named Guy Weadick was staging Calgary's first Stampede at the Elbow River fairgrounds, Sherman featured Fred Astaire and his sister Adele at the Sherman Grand. Astaire was only twelve at the time. Considered too young to head-line on Broadway, he toured Canada instead. The *Herald* character-ized the brother-sister act as "two clever youngsters who are compelled to stay indoors on a rainy day."

Sherman pulled off his biggest coup in January 1913, when he presented the great French actress Sarah Bernhardt at the Sherman Grand. Although she was then close to seventy, overweight, and forced to perform from a chair due to a knee injury, she still had enough gasoline in her tank to power her way through excerpts from Victor Hugo's *Lucrezia Borgia* and Alexandre Dumas' *La Dame aux Camélias*. Even the critics were impressed. "In her acting, there is nothing to suggest that her powers are in decline, or that she is aught still but the Divine Sarah," wrote the *Herald* reviewer, adding that while the majority of the audience couldn't understand French, "that did not distract from their interest in the piece. The personality of the great actress kept her audience enthralled."

American actress Maude Adams, who originated the role of Peter Pan on Broadway, and Blanche Bates, who made her name as the original Girl of the Golden West, followed Bernhardt at the Sherman Grand. By the middle of 1913, however, Calgary's first building boom was going bust and box office receipts at the Sherman Grand were dwindling. To compound his problems, Sherman found himself in court dealing with an accusation that he was a racist. A black Canadian Pacific Railway worker, Charles H. Daniel, had bought a reserved seat in the stalls for a touring production of *King Lear*, and when he arrived at the theatre he was refused admission because of his colour. Daniel sued Lougheed and Sherman for one thousand dollars in damages.

Lougheed was excused from the court case because he wasn't involved in the actual management of the theatre. Sherman appeared to answer the charge and was found guilty. He insisted to the court that he was not biased against black people, but the judge sided with Daniel. "I want coloured people to see my show as well as anybody else," protested Sherman, "but our audience objects very much." He added that black patrons had a choice of either sitting in the balcony, away from the white members of the audience, "or we refund them their money."

In April 1914, the Sherman Grand presented what was to be the last international production seen in Calgary for many years. Laurence Irving, the younger son of Sir Henry Irving, appeared with his wife, Mabel Hackney, in a presentation of *Typhoon*, just a month before the pair were drowned in the sinking of the *Empress of Ireland* in the Gulf of St. Lawrence. In late August, as the First World War started making it impossible for international artists to tour, the Sherman Grand closed its doors.

When the Grand reopened in 1915, Sherman was no longer the manager and his name was gone from the marquee. No longer able to make a living from the international touring circuit, he had moved to Vancouver and disappeared into obscurity. In his last years, he sold miscellaneous wares from a pushcart on the streets of Vancouver. He died there, penniless, in March 1934, at age sixty-six.

The Grand Theatre continued to operate as a venue for little theatre, concerts, public lectures, and political rallies until 1937, when a Calgary lawyer named Jack Barron purchased it and converted it into a movie house. The theatre was divided into two cinemas in the 1970s and went through further changes in the 1980s when it became the Showcase Grand. At the time of writing, in May 2002, it was home to an indoor golf centre, and its fate was uncertain. The building's owners wanted to demolish the structure and put up a high-rise office tower, while a valiant group of heritage preservationists fought to save the building from the wrecker's ball.

William "Wild Bill" Peyto

Mountain man

1868–1943

His name is everywhere in Banff National Park—on road signs, restaurants, saloons, and mountain features, all called Peyto in memory of a reclusive outdoorsman who shaved himself with a hunting knife and silenced alarm clocks with his gun.

Bill Peyto (pronounced "pea-toe") lived and worked in the Rocky Mountains from the late 1880s to the 1930s, with time out for military service in both the Boer War and the First World War. Raised in a farming district in what is now part of Greater London, Peyto left England for North America when he was a teenager. He felt his country was becoming too industrialized and he wanted to live in the Canadian wilderness. Travelling west from Halifax along the newly built Canadian Pacific Railway line in 1887, Peyto worked as a labourer for the CPR near Golden and did some prospecting for copper in the mountains. He then settled on a plot of land near Cochrane, where it seemed for a while that he might take up ranching. But Peyto preferred being in the mountains, prospecting, guiding, hunting, and trapping. He moved to Banff, acquired some property from the federal government, built a log cabin, and called it home.

During the 1890s, Peyto established himself as an accomplished mountain guide, horse outfitter, and packer, guiding tourists attracted by the romance of the Rockies. Climbers and hunters sought his services because he knew the terrain so well. In 1895, he led the first expedition up Mount Assiniboine, a peak they called the "Matterhorn of the Rockies." The climbers failed to reach the summit then, but Peyto returned six years later to coordinate the first successful ascent of the mountain. He didn't make it all the way to the top himself. Instead, he left the climbing party when it was about one

"Wild Bill" Peyto: "She's trying to poison me."
(GLENBOW ARCHIVES NA-2943-2)

thousand feet short of the 11,870-foot summit and went prospecting for minerals. When he returned a day later, he learned that the climbers, led by a British clergyman named Sir James Outram, had conquered the mountain. Peyto's packer celebrated by breaking out his fiddle and playing a chorus of "Hail the Conquering Hero Comes."

"Wild Bill," as Peyto now called himself, built a number of cabins in the mountains to serve as temporary shelters whenever he planned to spend an extended period in the backcountry. The most permanent of these was in Simpson Pass, near what is now the Sunshine Village ski resort. Peyto believed that the limestone rocks in the area were rich in copper, and he built the cabin as a place to stay while mining his claim. It began as a one-room shack and expanded over the years to include two additions, an anteroom and a horse corral. During that time, Peyto's reputation as a colourful eccentric with an odd sense of humour began to grow. One of his habits was to snowshoe from his copper claim into Banff, buy a steak at the butcher shop and make a big show of eating it raw while snowshoeing home. He refused to use a razor and always shaved himself— badly—with his hunting knife. It is also claimed that he killed a grizzly bear with his pistol, blew away an alarm clock with his gun because he didn't like the sound of the bell, and turned a lynx loose in a Banff saloon just to watch the drunken patrons scramble out of the way.

In 1899, Peyto tossed a coin with a fellow prospector to decide who would enlist for service in the Boer War and who would stay behind to maintain their copper claims. Peyto won the toss, joined Lord Strathcona's Horse Regiment, and found himself in South Africa acting as a mounted decoy whose job it was to ride alone ahead of his column and draw fire from the enemy. He did this for six months and, although he had two horses shot out from under him, Peyto was never hit. When he returned to his copper claim, he discovered that the man supposed to be looking after it had abandoned the claim to go prospecting for gold in South Africa. Peyto was not impressed. He installed a bear trap in his cabin as protection against would-be thieves and claim jumpers.

Peyto married Emily Wood in Banff in 1902 and they had a son named Robert. When Emily died suddenly in 1906, Peyto sent Robert to live with a cousin in British Columbia, and he returned to the backcountry to work his copper claim and prospect for talc. When a friend asked him about the loaded bear trap that he still kept in his cabin, Peyto replied, "An old trapper down the valley has been stealing my grub." The friend pointed out that if the trapper fell into the trap, he would likely die. "You're damn right he would," laughed Peyto. "Then I would have known for sure it was him."

His skills as a woodsman served him well. In 1913, Peyto became one of the first park wardens in what is now Banff National Park and was paid three dollars a day to patrol the vast rugged terrain surrounding his copper claim, protect wildlife, and catch poachers. He continued to build additional cabins as his park duties expanded to include trail-building. His park bosses soon appreciated that these structures were a necessity in the backcountry. Wardens were expected to travel over a wide area and they needed convenient housing along the way.

During the First World War, Peyto traded one government service for another. He served with the Twelfth Mounted Regiment and the Machine Gun Brigade in Belgium and France and was wounded in the right thigh by shellfire in the 1916 battle of Ypres. After a long convalescence in England, Peyto returned to the warden service, where his colleagues now included his younger brother Walter. Together, in the days before park wardens were prohibited from carrying sidearms, Bill and Walter became quite adept at shooting coyotes, an activity encouraged by park managers, who thought the predators should be killed to save deer and elk. Of the thirty-five coyotes killed by park wardens in one year, the Peyto brothers took twenty-five. They sold the pelts to augment their incomes.

The high point of Bill's career with the warden service occurred in 1921 when he helped rescue a Mrs. Winthrop Stone from a ledge on Mount Eon, in the Assiniboine area, after her husband fell to his death. Peyto received a commendation plaque from the American Alpine Club for his part in the rescue. That same year, he married Ethel Wells of Banff, a fellow Briton who tolerated his long absences—wardens were allowed only one day a month in town to obtain supplies—and, perhaps more important, his increasingly cranky ways. Among his peculiarities was a refusal to eat any food his wife left behind after she visited his wilderness cabin. "She's trying to poison me," he told an acquaintance.

During the late 1920s, the government introduced new rules for its national parks, decreeing that wardens should now only kill predators when they posed a danger to humans and that they should no longer keep the hides. Peyto fought the policy change because he believed it would have an adverse economic impact on wardens with families, and he began putting his cabins in places where he could not be found easily. He continued to shoot coyotes and mountain lions to earn what he saw as his entitlement and became like a ghost in the wilderness in his capacity as a law enforcer, suddenly appearing out of nowhere to warn suspected poachers that their presence was not wanted.

Peyto continued to do some prospecting and mining while working as a warden, but he doesn't seem to have gained much from this activity aside from a few fossils and mineral specimens that he sold to museums and private collectors. Besides, he didn't have much time for such extracurricular activity because the warden's job kept him busy seven days a week. On his personnel record, he wrote that he worked "an average of nineteen hours a day."

By 1930, Peyto was starting to slow down due to arthritis, age— he was then sixty-one—and the aggravation of his old war wound, which necessitated a two-week stay at Calgary's Colonel Belcher hospital for war veterans. He was granted another medical leave when he was thrown from his horse and suffered a further injury to the leg. In 1934, he was granted a year's exemption from his regular duties, with the understanding he would do "special work" controlling mountain lions and other predators. He was granted a further exemption in 1935 and finally retired from the warden service in 1936.

Peyto spent the next few years caring for his wife, Ethel, until she died in 1940 at age sixty-two. At that point, he was over seventy and, to the amazement of his friends, tried to enlist for service in the Second World War. Having served in two wars, the ever-patriotic Peyto felt he still had something to offer his country. Needless to say, his application was rejected. Peyto spent the years after that venturing into the wilderness as much as his health would allow. In early

1943 he told a friend that he had "a misery in my insides and my plumbing is out of order." He died of cancer at the Colonel Belcher hospital in March 1943 at age seventy-five.

Fifty years after Peyto's death, three park wardens accidentally discovered one of his hideaway cabins when they were tracking a wounded grizzly near Banff. Located on a ridge below Mount Bourgeau, it could only be reached by rope and was well sheltered from the elements. It contained a bed, cast-iron cooking stove, and an unopened can of food. "It was as if he planned to come back," said a Parks Canada officer, adding that Peyto likely built other shelters that will never be found.

Peyto's importance to the region is reflected in several ways: His craggy face adorns the sign that welcomes visitors at the entrance to the Banff townsite, and one of his cabins is protected—along with other examples of early town homes—on the grounds of the Whyte Museum of the Canadian Rockies. His name has been given to nearby Peyto Lake, Peyto Glacier, Peyto Peak, and—in a more commercial vein—to Wild Bill's Legendary Saloon, Peyto Place, and Bill Peyto's Café. His name and picture have also been adopted by a Calgary oil and gas company, Peyto Exploration and Development, which seems somehow appropriate for a company that hopes—as Peyto did—to find riches in the wilderness.

Emilio "Emperor Pic" Picariello

Bootlegger and convicted murderer

1879–1923

~

Florence Lassandro

Bootlegger's accomplice and convicted murderer

1900–1923

One of Alberta's most notorious murder cases of the 1920s occurred in the Crowsnest Pass in 1922, when Prohibition was in full force. It involved the gunning down in broad daylight of a provincial police officer assigned to combat illicit liquor traffic in the towns of Blairmore, Bellevue, and Coleman. Two suspects were convicted and sentenced to death. One was a rum-runner named Emilio Picariello who had vowed to kill the policeman for shooting at his son. The other was his female accomplice, Florence Lassandro, a Picariello family friend. Lassandro considered herself innocent yet still took the blame for the policeman's killing because Picariello had told her that Canadian judicial authorities would never execute a woman.

She was just twenty-two when she went to the gallows. Born Filumena Costanzo in Calabria, Italy, Lassandro immigrated to Canada with her family in 1909, when she was nine years old, and settled in Fernie, British Columbia, where her father worked initially as a railway labourer and then as a coal miner. One of her school-teachers anglicized her first name to Florence, telling her the name meant "flower." The young girl, who loved wildflowers, happily embraced her new name.

When Lassandro was fourteen, her parents arranged for her to be married—against her will—to Carlo Sanfidele, a twenty-three-year-old Italian immigrant who worked for Emilio Picariello as a travelling salesman, hawking cigars and ice cream in the border towns on either side of the British Columbia-Alberta boundary. Local legend says that Picariello, as Sanfidele's boss and best man and godfather of the working-class Italians in southeastern British Columbia, was allowed to bed Lassandro on her wedding night. Picariello hosted the wedding celebration at his house in Fernie and gave the bridal couple one of his bedrooms for the night.

Picariello, born in Italy, had immigrated to Canada in 1899 at age twenty, settled in Toronto, saved his money from various labouring jobs, and opened a grocery store specializing in Italian foods. In 1900 he married Maria Marucci, a fellow immigrant who worked as a housekeeper at a Toronto boarding house. A year later, their son, Stefano, was born. At that point, Picariello decided to move with his family to Fernie, where there was a sizable Italian immigrant population, and try his luck as a merchant. He rented an old macaroni factory, hired women to roll cigars for him, and hired Sanfidele to sell them. Picariello subsequently expanded into ice cream manufacturing and liquor bottle recycling, taking the bottles as payment for his ice cream cones and selling the bottles to British Columbia distillers and breweries. As his business grew, so did his prominence. He weighed two hundred pounds, had a fierce, bristling moustache, and was known locally as "Emperor Pic, the Bottle King," who "requests that all persons selling bottles hold them until they see E. Picariello, who pays top prices."

Sanfidele quit his job with Picariello shortly after marrying Lassandro and briefly moved with her to Pennsylvania, where he hoped to become one of those successful Italian immigrants who wore new suits, silk shirts, and big diamonds on their fingers. After a few months in the States, where Sanfidele consorted with mobsters, they returned to Fernie. Sanfidele was by now calling himself Charles Lassandro. He had entered the United States illegally and hoped to hide back in Canada under an assumed name. He would later be deported back to Italy.

Lassandro went back to work for Picariello, who had switched from cigars and ice cream to bootlegging. The year was 1916, and

"Emperor Pic" Picariello: "If they will use guns, then so do we."
(GLENBOW ARCHIVES NA-3282-1)

Prohibition was in force in Alberta—though not yet in British Columbia. Under the circumstances, it became inevitable that the Crowsnest Pass route between "wet" British Columbia and "dry" Alberta would become a bootlegger's trail. Prohibition enhanced rather than prevented thirst. Picariello was quick to see the demand for liquor in towns throughout the pass where mining was the chief occupation. He didn't worry about being caught by the North-West Mounted Police. The proceeds from just one case of Scotch or rye whisky would cover the fine, he figured, and the rest would end up in his pockets as profit.

When British Columbia adopted Prohibition in 1917, Picariello decided to move to the Alberta side of the border. He wanted a place that was central to the bootlegging trade, close to "wet" Montana, but not too far from the barnyard distilleries of British Columbia. When he saw the Alberta Hotel in Blairmore, he knew it was just the building he needed for his operations. From this hotel, Emperor Pic would direct some of the most daring north-south liquor runs ever staged in the history of western Canadian bootlegging.

Picariello engaged Charles Lassandro to work for him as hotel manager and he put Florence to work in his dining room, waiting on tables. In the hotel basement, he built a garage for the three McLaughlin six-cylinder touring cars that he planned to use for running booze from Fernie, eastward via the Crowsnest Pass, to the border crossing at Sweetgrass, Montana. He hired a mechanic to keep the cars serviced and recruited two drivers to assist him with the liquor runs.

In 1918 the Alberta government, in an effort to stem the illicit flow of booze through the Crowsnest Pass, stationed detachments of its newly established provincial police in Blairmore, Bellevue, and Coleman. Under federal law, it was still legal to ship liquor from British Columbia to the United States. But it could not be brought legally into Alberta, which was the only route by road from Fernie to Sweetgrass.

The Alberta police set up a system of checkpoints and roadblocks to catch the rum-runners. Whenever police in one Crowsnest detachment spotted a suspicious-looking car speeding eastward through the pass, they would phone ahead to the next detachment to have the rum-runner intercepted. In theory, this should have resulted in many arrests because there were hardly any side roads that the rum-runners could use as effective escape routes. But the rum-runners had their warning spies too, and so it became a relatively simple matter for them to slip through the net whenever the police were either otherwise engaged or off duty. As a result, few arrests were made and fewer convictions registered.

One method Picariello used to evade capture was to have two cars drive in convoy on the liquor run from British Columbia to Montana. The first one would drive empty as a decoy, while the liquor-loaded car followed behind. If the pilot-car driver encountered a police checkpoint, he would cause enough of an obstruction for the other driver to reverse direction and speed back to the safety of the Alberta-British Columbia border.

Another of Picariello's methods was to have his teenaged son, Stefano (Steve), drive the decoy car with Florence beside him in the passenger seat. If stopped by the police, Steve would say they were an engaged couple either heading out to or coming back from a picnic. The resulting distraction would allow the loaded second car to pass right through the checkpoint without hindrance. It was an effective strategy, but it didn't sit too well with Florence's husband, Charles. He couldn't stand the thought of his wife masquerading as another man's fiancée.

Florence rode with the bootleggers for several years, sometimes with Picariello or his son, sometimes with the other drivers. Occasionally she drove herself, at speeds of up to fifty miles an hour. Charles grew increasingly jealous, and eventually she separated from him and moved into her own room in the Blairmore hotel. Emperor Pic grew rich and obtained a magistrate's permit to possess and carry a handgun. He told the magistrate that because he carried large sums of money whenever he travelled from Blairmore to Fernie on his "business trips," he needed a gun to protect himself from robbery.

By 1920, Emperor Pic was one of the Crowsnest Pass area's most influential citizens, seen by the citizens as a kind of Robin Hood or benevolent godfather. At Christmastime, he dispensed packages filled with fruit, candy, and other goodies to the poor of the area, and he entertained local children at special motion picture shows. He ran for alderman of Blairmore and was elected by a large majority, solidly supported by the Italian immigrant vote.

As a bootlegger, Picariello was part of a province-wide underground industry estimated to generate more than $7 million annually. Statistics claimed that as many as sixty-five percent of the Alberta population regularly broke the liquor laws, and abuses were widespread. Stories abounded of judges and lawyers getting drunk before dealing with liquor-act violators. Doctors and druggists, who were licensed to write prescriptions for "medicinal" beverages, made small fortunes. Men returning from the First World War were angry at the prohibitionists who had opposed both tobacco and liquor for servicemen. The government, caught in the middle between the irate "wet" side and the defensive "dry" side, could only grimace.

The provincial police constantly monitored Picariello's movements as they endeavoured to enforce the Alberta Liquor Act. In January 1922, they seized seventy cases of beer from a railway car in Blairmore and charged Picariello with unlawfully keeping liquor for sale because the bill of lading was in his name. Picariello tried to argue that he had ordered a shipment of carbonated water, not beer, from the Fernie Brewery, but the judge found him guilty and fined him five hundred dollars.

Picariello dismissed the fine as "business expenses," but it was only the start of his troubles. On September 21, 1922, he and his son ran afoul of the police as they came back from a liquor run to Fernie in two cars. The elder Picariello, driving the empty pilot car, blocked the road in an effort to stop the Blairmore police from catching Steve as he retreated back to Fernie with the loaded car. The Blairmore police phoned back to the Coleman detachment, and a constable there named Steve Lawson tried to stop the younger Picariello by firing a couple of shots in the air. When that failed, Lawson commandeered a car, gave chase, tracked his quarry to within gun range, and fired another shot. It struck Steve Picariello in the hand but he carried on driving. Constable Lawson was forced to give up the chase when his car blew a tire, and Steve made it safely back to Fernie.

The elder Picariello went home to his hotel in Blairmore, where the report of the Coleman shooting drifted back to him in a garbled version. He knew only that his son had been wounded, not how badly. He vowed revenge against Lawson when told who fired the shot. "If he did [shoot Steve], I would kill him," said Picariello. Back in Coleman, Constable Lawson went home to the barracks and had supper with his wife and five children.

Picariello decided to drive to Coleman to confront Lawson. "If they will use guns, then so do we," he told his wife, Maria. She begged him not to go, but Picariello was determined. "I'm going to see him, he hurt my son." Florence offered to accompany him. Later she would tell the police that she wanted to go with Picariello because she "liked Steve." She added that she didn't want her husband to know about this. That was as close as the record ever got to identifying Florence's actual relationship with the Picariello family.

At the outskirts of Coleman, Picariello pulled a .38-calibre revolver from under his coat and placed it in his lap. He handed another gun, a .32-calibre automatic, to Florence. "For protection," he said. "They used guns this afternoon." He stopped the car outside the police barracks. Lawson's wife saw the vehicle pull up and called her husband to the front door. He went outside and spent the next several minutes talking to the occupants of the car.

The conversation turned into a physical confrontation. Witnesses saw Lawson standing on the car's running board, grappling with Picariello, with his arms firmly wrapped around the bootlegger's neck. Two shots were fired. One shattered the speedometer glass and the other went through the windshield. The unarmed Lawson loosened his hold on Picariello, turned, and started to run toward the barracks. Two more shots were fired. Lawson fell mortally wounded in the street with a bullet in his back. The car roared to life, cut across a vacant lot in front of the police barracks, and sped eastward along the main street.

Lawson's nine-year-old daughter witnessed the incident from outside the barracks. Her mother responded to her screams, saw her husband lying in the street, and ran toward him, while a neighbour ran for the doctor. The first shots had attracted the attention of several bystanders, and all of them were able to testify as witnesses at the subsequent trial.

The two fugitives did not return to the hotel in Blairmore, but spent the night hiding in an abandoned shack. The next day

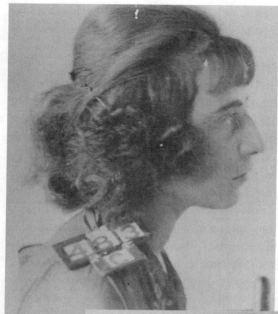

Police mug shots of
Florence Lassandro:
"Why do you hang
me when I didn't do
anything?"
(GLENBOW ARCHIVES
NA-3282-2)

Picariello took off on foot into the hills above the town, while Florence sought refuge in the home of a woman friend. Police officers from Lethbridge and Edmonton travelled by train to the Crowsnest Pass to join the manhunt. They found Picariello in the mountains, and he quickly surrendered. "How is my boy? Is he dead?" asked Picariello. "No," answered an officer, "just shot in the hand." When the officer added that Lawson was dead, Picariello said nothing. Florence was arrested shortly afterwards, following an anonymous tip to the police barracks in Blairmore. A joint charge of murder was laid. Because there was no courtroom large enough to accommodate the expected crowds, the arraignment took place in the Coleman opera house. The trial was set for Fort Macleod.

The case sparked a frenzy of lurid coverage in newspapers across Alberta. The two accused were described as "foreigners" engaged in a lucrative bootlegging business in southern Alberta. Picariello was said to be the leader of a gang of rum-runners who made untold amounts of money from the illicit trade. Florence was described variously as the Emperor Pic's adopted daughter, his daughter-in-law, and—in one instance—his mistress. Press coverage was so extensive that when a motion was made to move the trial from Fort Macleod to Calgary, it was quickly granted.

The Calgary press coverage differed little from the accounts published in other parts of the province. In fact, the Calgary coverage was so extensive on the eve of the trial that Mr. Justice William Walsh, who presided, criticized it as irresponsible and potentially prejudicial. So great was the public interest in the case that Judge Walsh on several occasions had to order the corridors outside the courtroom cleared of noisy crowds to let the hearing proceed.

When the trial opened on November 27, 1922, John E. Brownlee, the attorney general of Alberta, appeared in court to lay the murder charge against the two accused. Moreover, he remained for the entire five-day trial. This was the first time in Alberta history that any attorney general had taken such action, and it sent a clear message to the jury that the government was going to take a direct and aggressive part in asserting the rule of law in Alberta. The defence team was led by McKinley Cameron of Calgary, one of the best criminal lawyers in western Canada.

The jury heard the testimony of more than thirty prosecution witnesses. Several identified Emperor Pic and Florence Lassandro as the occupants of the car that stopped at the Coleman police barracks the night that Lawson was killed. Three testified that they saw Picariello brandishing a handgun outside the Blairmore hotel and heard him say, "If they have shot my boy, I will kill every policeman in the pass." The most damaging testimony came from Lawson's nine-year-old daughter, who said that she watched from the corner of the barracks and saw Florence fire a shot before her father loosened his grip on Picariello. The girl did not, however, see who fired the fatal shot. A police sergeant named J.O. Scott added to the girl's testimony by saying that Florence confessed to him, upon her arrest, that she had fired the fatal shot. But Scott admitted under cross-examination that he had not taken any notes of the conversation. Nor had he extracted a written confession.

The defence lawyers called no witnesses, and neither accused took the stand. Chief prosecutor A.A. McGillivray, in his summation to the jury, said there was evidence to show that while Picariello and Lassandro were in hiding they agreed that she would shoulder the blame, saying she shot in self-defence. But, noted McGillivray, "Lawson was shot in the back while moving away from bullets fired by these people. They could not have been defending themselves."

Defence lawyer Cameron insisted the self-defence theory was valid. Picariello had gone to Coleman simply to inquire about his son's well-being, not to kill Lawson. The constable had responded by grabbing Picariello around the neck, "probably choking him," and Florence had no choice but to use the gun to protect herself. "There was no trace of a plan," said Cameron. "There was no evidence of a common design to kill on the part of the accused." He asked the jury not to be "bullied or influenced" by the presence in the courtroom of Attorney General Brownlee and not to be swayed by the prosecution's attempt to "vindicate the virtues of the Alberta Liquor Act." "Give this man [Picariello] the same consideration as you would your neighbour or friend."

The jury retired shortly before 4 P.M. on Saturday, December 2. After a supper adjournment, the court resumed at 8 P.M., and the jury found both accused guilty of murder as charged. "You have reached the only possible verdict under the evidence given," said Mr. Justice Walsh, and he sentenced Picariello and Lassandro to be hanged on February 21, 1923.

Cameron appealed to the Supreme Court of Canada, asking that a verdict of manslaughter be rendered, but to no avail. That left the fate of Picariello and Lassandro up to Prime Minister W.L. Mackenzie King, who was bombarded with petitions and letters urging that the sentence of Lassandro be commuted to life imprisonment. The thought of a woman being hanged was just too much for many Canadians to bear. The prime minister also received two letters urging the government to proceed with the execution. One was from the Lawson family in Coleman. The other was from Magistrate Emily Murphy of Edmonton. Murphy would later achieve fame as one of the Famous Five who won the right to have Canadian women legally recognized as "persons" and thus eligible for Senate appointments.

On May 2, 1923, after two brief reprieves, Picariello and Lassandro were hanged. Picariello was given two ounces of whisky to drink and went to his death, at age forty-three, without uttering a word. Lassandro asked for a bouquet of lilies (which never arrived) and received a shot of morphine as well as the two ounces of whisky. She went to her death, at age twenty-two, protesting her innocence. "Picariello, he lied," she said to the priest who attended the execution. "I didn't hurt anyone, ever. I will not forgive any of you for doing this to me. Why do you hang me when I didn't do anything? Is there anyone here who has any pity?" The bodies of both accused were buried in separate unmarked graves in one of Edmonton's Catholic cemeteries.

Defence lawyer Cameron was roundly criticized by his fellow barristers for his handling of the case. Why had he not insisted that the two accused be tried separately? This, said the barristers, would have resulted in two verdicts and possibly a different outcome. Cameron might have won a not-guilty or a manslaughter verdict in Picariello's case by arguing that the rum-runner was being held down by Lawson when the first shot was fired, and that therefore Picariello could not have been guilty of premeditated murder. In the Lassandro case, Cameron could have argued that the pulling of the trigger was simply the act of a frightened woman, and that such an act amounted to manslaughter, not murder.

Cameron replied that he had had no choice. "Trying them separately was what I wanted to do," he said, "but Picariello would not stand for it. He said it was he who got Florence Lassandro into the mess, and he was not going to save himself by letting her be convicted, even of manslaughter." Cameron said he was left with no alternative but to create as much confusion as he could in the minds of the jurors, and hope that the doubts raised would result in a lesser verdict.

Alberta's eight-year experiment with Prohibition officially ended six months after Picariello and Lassandro were hanged. The sensational murder case had added to Albertans' mounting disenchantment with Prohibition, and the provincial government came under increasing pressure to modify or scrap its policy. The government's liquor legislation, it was argued, was the root cause of a tragedy that had resulted in the deaths of the provincial policeman and the two bootleggers. Adding impetus to the changing mood was the fact that British Columbia was earning a profit of a million dollars a year from its liquor stores. When a referendum was held, the people of Alberta voted to follow British Columbia's lead. On May 10, 1924, the first government liquor stores opened for business in Alberta. The enabling legislation was drafted by Attorney General Brownlee. They operated until 1993, when Premier Ralph Klein's government closed all 210 stores to save $67 million in annual operating costs.

Postscript

Florence Lassandro was the only woman ever hanged in Alberta and the last woman hanged in Canada. This has made her a continuing source of fascination for some Alberta authors, including this one. In 1983, her fate provided the inspiration for Sharon Pollock's play, *Whiskey Six*, in which the young woman was portrayed as the mistress of a Blairmore hotelier and booze smuggler named "Mr. Big." Lassandro was also the subject of Jock Carpenter's 1993 book, *The Bootlegger's Bride*, an exhaustively documented and partially fictionalized treatment of the murder case. And in 2001, the Banff Centre and Calgary Opera jointly announced that the story of Lassandro and Picariello would be retold in an opera called *Filumena*, by composer John Estacio and librettist John Murrell. Developed at a cost of $1.3 million, it was scheduled to receive its world premiere in Calgary in January 2003. "The combination of tragedy, murder, unrequited love, and larger-than-life emotions makes this story ideal for the opera," said composer Estacio.

Ernest Cashel

Outlaw

1882–1904

Ernest Cashel was nothing more than a two-bit criminal with a record of larceny and forgery when he first arrived in Alberta in late 1901. But thanks to an inept police chief who let him escape custody while being transported to Calgary to face a forgery charge, Cashel graduated from petty crime to murder in short order. And thanks to three bungling jail guards who let him escape custody again while awaiting execution for the murder, he wrote his name in the history books as one of Canada's most notorious desperadoes of the early twentieth century.

Born in Kansas and strongly influenced by the lore of the American Wild West, Cashel began his criminal career at age fourteen, when his single mother abandoned her three children and moved north to Ponoka, Alberta, to work as a cook in a lumber camp. Ernest, the middle child, drifted from state to state, trying to create for himself the romance of the outlaw life by gambling, cheating, and stealing. By the time he was sixteen, he had spent one year behind bars for larceny, and by the time he was nineteen, he was making a reputation for himself as an escape artist.

In the summer of 1901, Cashel broke loose from a prison in Buffalo, Wyoming, where he was serving two years for larceny. He fled to Kansas and was arrested three months later. But before he could be returned to Buffalo to finish his sentence, he escaped again. This time, Cashel fled north to Ponoka to hide out at his mother's place. From there he moved south to the Shepard area, east of Calgary, where he briefly worked as a ranch hand.

In late 1902, Cashel moved into Calgary and tried making a living as a barber. When that failed, he started forging cheques. A city storekeeper offered a good description of the forger to the police, and

Calgary's police chief, Thomas English, assumed charge of the case. When he asked the North-West Mounted Police for assistance, they reported back that a man answering Cashel's description—slight, dark-haired, and about twenty years old—was seen working at a ranch near Ponoka. A Mountie stationed in Red Deer was dispatched to apprehend the fugitive, and Chief English travelled north to assist in the arrest and escort the prisoner back to Calgary by train. Cashel gave up without a struggle. The arresting officers secured him with leg irons and handcuffs. The leg irons stayed on until the train reached Red Deer, when Chief English removed them so that Cashel could accompany him to a local restaurant for dinner.

On October 18, 1902, Albertans read in their daily newspapers that the young American had escaped from custody—"the first person the chief ever lost." Using the oldest ruse in the outlaw's handbook, Cashel had asked permission to use the train's washroom. The gullible chief, charmed by the small talk of a man he considered to be a model prisoner, removed the handcuffs and waited at the washroom door until he realized that Cashel wasn't coming out. He forced open the door and found Cashel's topcoat and vest on the floor but no sign of the prisoner. Cashel had climbed out the washroom window and jumped, "even though the train was going about twenty miles an hour."

One week later, a man answering Cashel's description showed up at a farmhouse near Lacombe, gave his name as Bert Ellsworth, and said he had been thrown from his horse, which then ran off with his coat and gloves. The farmer and his wife put up the soft-spoken stranger for the night and lent him some clothes and a pony with the understanding that "Ellsworth" would return them the next day. When he hadn't reappeared after a week, the farmer reported the incident to the mounted police. By then Cashel had found shelter thirty-eight miles east of Lacombe with an unsuspecting Kansas-born homesteader named Isaac Rufus Belt.

On November 1, 1902, Cashel traded in a saddle and bridle and paid ten dollars cash for a horse and cart in Lacombe. The saddle had the name "I.R. Belt" printed in ink on it. Three weeks later, on November 19, Belt's brother-in-law reported to police that the homesteader was missing. Also missing were Belt's pony, some clothing, a

Outlaw Ernest Cashel: "Don't do anything boys,
you are afraid to let your mother know."
(GLENBOW ARCHIVES NA-1528-1)

shotgun, and about fifty dollars in cash. Fearing foul play, the mounted police assigned one of their best investigators, Constable Alexander Pennycuick, to take charge of the case. Over the next few weeks, police received reports of several Cashel sightings, one of which took Pennycuick as far south as Prineville, Oregon. The constable referred to his elusive quarry as "this crimson disciple of Jesse James."

Shortly before Christmas, Cashel arrived by horse and cart at the Sarcee reserve near Calgary. He was now using the alias Nick Carter, a pseudonym used by the authors of the dime-store crime novels he had read as a youth. He persuaded two Native boys to buy ammunition and clothing for him, and then he headed west toward the mountains. When his horse went lame, Cashel stopped at the home of Jumping Pound rancher Glen Healy and borrowed another— ostensibly to catch his own horse, which he said had strayed. When Cashel failed to return the horse, Healy notified police.

Cashel carried on to Kananaskis, abandoned Healy's horse, broke into a woman's house, stole her diamond ring, and hopped a freight train to Canmore. From there, he made his way to Anthracite, a coal-mining town near Banff that existed from 1886 to 1904. Police took up the chase when Cashel cashed a cheque at the Anthracite railway station and was recognized by the stationmaster. Finally, on January 24, 1903, the police net enveloped Cashel. Police arrested him at his Anthracite boarding house, brought him to Calgary, and lodged him in the mounted police barracks. At the time of his arrest, he was carrying the woman's diamond ring and wearing a pair of corduroy pants that strongly resembled a pair owned by the missing Lacombe rancher, Isaac Rufus Belt.

Although Constable Pennycuick believed Cashel had caused the disappearance of Belt, he had no proof because there was no body. So when Cashel appeared in a Calgary court on May 14, 1903, he was charged only with the theft of Glen Healy's horse and the Kananaskis woman's ring. The judge convicted him and sentenced him to three years of hard labour at Manitoba's Stony Mountain penitentiary.

The search for Belt continued through the summer of 1903. On July 20, a farmer living downstream from Belt's cabin noticed a corpse floating in the Red Deer River. A deformed toe identified the body as that of Belt, and a .44-calibre bullet extracted from the chest matched bullets taken from Cashel's gun at the time of his arrest. A coroner's jury reported that Belt "came to his death from murder and, in our opinion, by the hand of one Cashel, now in Stony Mountain penitentiary." Police brought Cashel back to Calgary in October to face the murder charge. After an eight-day trial, he was found guilty and sentenced to be hanged on December 15, 1903. The jury took just thirty-five minutes to deliver its verdict.

That should have been the end of the story, but there was one more chapter yet to unfold. During the weeks leading up to the execution, stories started circulating in Calgary that mobsters from Wyoming were heading north to spring Cashel from custody. Some were said to be from the notorious Hole-in-the-Wall gang, which boasted the outlaw Butch Cassidy as a member. As it turned out, the only visitor from Wyoming was Cashel's brother John, who arrived ostensibly to bring condolences from the family. Instead, he brought two loaded revolvers that he slipped through the bars to Cashel when the guards were looking the other way. John then departed and when the three police guards were eating supper, Ernest Cashel pointed the pistols at them and ordered them to unlock his cell door. He herded the guards into the cell, locked it, and then calmly undid his shackles and walked out into the night. "Goodbye, boys," he said as he left.

Police immediately launched what the *Calgary Daily Herald* described as "the greatest manhunt in the history of the Territories." Officers from Banff to Maple Creek, in what is now Saskatchewan, were ordered to drop everything and take part in the search. A reward of one thousand dollars was offered for Cashel, "dead or alive." His defence lawyer, Paddy Nolan, who was in Ottawa pleading for a new trial, remarked to the minister of justice, "We may not need a new trial."

Cashel remained on the run for forty-five days. His brother was picked up almost immediately and charged with aiding and abetting. The three constables who allowed the escape were dealt with summarily. One was sentenced to one year of hard labour, and the other two men to six months each. All were ordered dismissed from the force at the end of their sentences. This prompted one of their former colleagues to write a protest letter to the *Herald*: "Chief English allowed Ernest Cashel to escape from the train near Red Deer, yet he did not get a year's imprisonment. Had Cashel not escaped in the first place, Rufus Belt would never have been murdered."

While the manhunt ranged across the western prairies and down into the United States, Cashel stayed close to Calgary, perhaps with the idea that he might help his brother escape. He was spotted several times but never by the police. He continued to steal money, horses, and clothing from area ranches. In one instance, he left a note saying he would return the stolen items in six months. He signed the note "Ernest Cashel." In another instance, he sent a letter written on hotel stationery to a Calgary priest suggesting that the public hangman be sent home because "I expect to live a little longer." Cashel added that he had plenty of friends, was very comfortable, read the *Herald* every day, and knew everything that was going on.

Police finally tracked Cashel to his lair on January 24, 1904. Acting on a tip, forty officers and citizen volunteers surrounded a farmhouse seven miles east of Calgary, where Cashel was said to be hiding in a haystack. They found him in the cellar of the farmhouse, exchanged shots with him, and threatened to burn down the house if he didn't surrender. "I don't want to be roasted," he replied, and came out with his hands up.

The *Herald,* which at the request of police had stopped printing day-to-day updates on the manhunt, published a special edition to celebrate the recapture of the fugitive. "Graphic story of the most sensational case in the history of Canada," said the headline. "Surrounded by posse and driven out by fire."

Cashel was hanged nine days later, on February 2, 1904. Before going to the gallows, he confessed to a priest that he was guilty. Two men were jailed for sheltering Cashel while he was on the run. The reward money went to the volunteers who took part in the final raid. Constable Pennycuick, promoted to corporal for his detective work on the case, was demoted to constable again after he registered at a Vancouver hotel as a commercial traveller, became drunk and disorderly in the hotel bar, and then was charged with being a deserter from the mounted police. In a macabre final twist to the story, the public hangman set up shop in a Calgary hotel bar immediately after the execution and sold souvenir pieces of the execution rope at twenty-five cents apiece. He told the bar patrons he needed the extra money for expenses.

Postscript

Sixty years after Cashel's execution, someone found his death note and donated it to the Glenbow Museum archives in Calgary. Addressed as "advice to young men," it warned of the perils of "saloons, gambling houses, and the houses of ill-fame" and said that crime novels were the worst influence of all. "Stay at home, shun novels, bad company and cigarettes," it concluded. "Don't do anything, boys, you are afraid to let your mother know."

Cashel was twenty-one when he went to the gallows.

Pearl Miller

Brothel keeper

1882–1957

The best-known story about the most famous madam in Calgary history is a fiction that has endured for more than half a century. It tells how a group of Calgary soldiers—who could have been members of the Calgary Highlanders or could have been members of Princess Patricia's Canadian Light Infantry—camped next to a regiment of American soldiers on the eve of the Normandy invasion in 1944. The Americans, who were fond of slogans, tacked up a sign on the wall of their sergeants' mess that read, "Remember Pearl Harbor." The Calgarians responded by putting up their own sign: "To hell with Pearl Harbour, remember Pearl Miller."

More than a dozen Calgary veterans subsequently swore that the episode occurred—even to the point of saying they actually saw the signs—this despite the fact that the story was a complete fabrication. But truth is irrelevant in this instance because, as social historian James H. Gray noted in an early draft of his 1971 book about prostitution, *Red Lights on the Prairies*, the Pearl Miller story has the fundamental qualities of a legend. "It could have happened. It should have happened. A great many people believe it did happen. In order to get a flat lie promoted to legend status, it must be repeated frequently." The Miller story was repeated so often, in newspaper stories and popular histories, that eventually it developed enough momentum of its own to remain in circulation indefinitely.

Who was Pearl Miller? Historian Gray, who knew more about whoring on the Prairies than any social studies expert around, was unable able to find out much about her when he did his research for *Red Lights*. One can easily understand why. Prostitutes were not given to issuing press releases or granting interviews to the popular press.

Pearl Miller, for all her notoriety, was rarely in the public eye. Stories about her didn't start appearing in local newspapers until long after her death.

Gray did learn, from former Miller clients who spoke on condition of anonymity, that she was an American who settled in Rossland, British Columbia, around the turn of the twentieth century and married a man there named Rose. He disappeared from her life soon afterwards, but she kept his last name for legal purposes. She moved to Calgary just before the First World War and worked as a prostitute in the brothels along east-side Sixth Avenue downtown. In 1914, she was arrested and charged with vagrancy—a common complaint laid against itinerant prostitutes. The police mug shot shows her to be a dark-haired, dark-eyed, sallow-skinned woman who looked to be of Spanish or Italian ancestry. She paid the fine and carried on working in Calgary's red-light district.

By 1926, Miller had earned enough from prostitution to open her own brothel in a bungalow at 526 Ninth Avenue S.E., opposite the railway tracks half a block east of where the King Edward Hotel is today. She operated out of there until 1929, when a rich client— identified by historian Gray as "the son of one of Calgary's most prominent lawyers"—set her up in a big fieldstone house south of the city limits, near the intersection of the present Macleod Trail and Heritage Drive. This house soon became the most famous brothel in Alberta, catering to a high-class clientele. It was never raided by police, who confined their law-enforcement activities to within the city boundary.

Oilmen en route to Turner Valley and back regularly stopped off at Miller's establishment for a drink, sex, and sometimes a game of bridge with Miller and her current lover. She was typical among Calgary madams in that she operated more like a den mother than a brothel-keeper, but unusual in that she kept a cleaner and better-furnished place than the sordid brothels in the downtown core. Men imagined they were sitting in a respectable parlour courting the girls rather than paying for sex. One of Miller's frequent customers recalled that the atmosphere was always pleasant and cheerful. "There was never much rowdiness, even though her place was often full of Turner Valley roughnecks. She really acted more like a hostess than a whore. She'd visit with you and have a drink with you, though I never saw her drunk. She kept her eye on her girls and tried to run a real nice place where you liked to return to. If you didn't know or didn't think where you were, you could easily get over what kind of house it was. In that case, you could imagine you were in a third-class boarding house parlour with ordinary lodgers, with Pearl being the landlady looking after things."

Miller did so well catering to what she called the "carriage trade"—that is, those with ample financial means—that in 1935 she boldly relocated to 1813 Ninth Street S.W., at the lower end of Mount Royal, Calgary's most exclusive residential district. "It too was a great life while it lasted," wrote historian Gray. Miller made it last until 1939, when police, responding to complaints from neighbours, raided the house and charged her with keeping liquor for sale. One of the arresting officers noted that the house was "quite tastefully furnished. It didn't look cheap or gaudy, like some of these bordellos can be." Six weeks later, police raided the house again, this time to charge Miller with keeping a common bawdy house. She paid a heavy fine, moved her business out of lower Mount Royal, and reopened the brothel in her bungalow on Ninth Avenue S.E.

In 1941, Miller's long career as Calgary's most famous madam finally came to an end. Police constables Jock Ritchie and Harry Timms, who had spent many cold hours conducting surveillance on Miller's house from an empty boxcar—and had even suffered the embarrassment of being stuck in the boxcar when a trainman innocently connected it to a locomotive and towed it out of town— finally amassed enough evidence to charge Miller again with keeping a common bawdy house. This time she had no option of paying a fine. Three convictions in as many years were enough to satisfy the judge that Miller should be sent to the Fort Saskatchewan jail for three months.

Constable Ritchie recalled afterwards that Miller was extremely polite in her dealings with the police. "She seemed to take it for granted that you were on the one side of the fence, and she was on the other—that we had a job to do—and she never seemed to bear any grudges against us. Of course, I think she was fairly treated according to the rules. Even after she went out of the bawdy house business, if I met her on the street, she would speak in passing. She never seemed to bear any ill-will against us."

Miller seems to have found religion while serving her three-month jail sentence. When she emerged from Fort Saskatchewan in 1942, she closed up her Ninth Avenue house—which has since been demolished—returned to her home in lower Mount Royal, and spent the last fifteen years of her life attempting to salvage young women from prostitution. According to historian Gray, "If she happened to be in the neighbourhood after a police raid on one of the brothels, she would wander up to the jail, pass the time with the jailers, and try to get at the girls while they were in a receptive mood to be reformed." How successful she was is not known, but it is known that her fame as a prostitute was destined to live on long after her efforts as a social worker were forgotten.

Miller died in 1957, at age seventy-five. Her lower Mount Royal house was later knocked down to make way for a residential health care centre. Nineteen years after her death, Calgary's Lunchbox Theatre presented a one-act musical, *Remember Pearl Miller,* which was loosely based on the Gray book and elevated Miller to the status of folk heroine. Librettist Bartley Bard gave one of the prostitute characters the name "Sadie" to rhyme with the word "lady" in her first song. A man in the Lunchbox audience—who claimed to have known Miller, though not as a client—subsequently told Bard that Miller's most popular prostitute was, in fact, named Sadie Bushmill. Truth or fiction? It hardly matters now. A good legend is always in need of a little embellishment.

John Edward Brownlee

Fallen premier

1883–1961

~

Vivian MacMillan

Government stenographer

1912–1980

As political sex scandals go, it seemed like pretty tame stuff at first. When a junior government stenographer named Vivian MacMillan in 1933 accused Alberta premier John E. Brownlee of sexual misconduct, the province's newspapers devoted less coverage to the civil lawsuit than they did to a juicy wife-swapping suit involving Brownlee's public works minister, O.L. (Tony) McPherson. But when the stenographer's charges stuck and the fifty-year-old premier had to publicly defend himself in court, the newspapers broke out the big black headlines that they normally reserve for coverage of a world war. It was cheap entertainment for the Depression-battered masses, and they devoured it with prurient relish.

Brownlee was reaching the peak of his career in politics when MacMillan's accusations undermined him. Provincial premiers across Canada applauded him for wresting control of Alberta's natural resources away from Ottawa—a move that later allowed the province to evolve into a powerful economic force—and for drafting the legislation that ended Prohibition in Alberta. Prime Minister R.B. Bennett honoured Brownlee by appointing him to a Royal Commission on banking that created the corporate structure for the Bank of Canada. From humble beginnings, Brownlee travelled far.

Fallen premier John E. Brownlee: "She was like a member of the family. I would say like a niece." (GLENBOW ARCHIVES NA-1451-11)

His journey was dotted with ironies and paradoxes. A native of Ontario, he became a determined and committed defender of Alberta's economic rights. A lawyer who never farmed, he became the dominant political figure in the United Farmers of Alberta during the fourteen years that the farmers' party ruled as the government of Alberta, and he always managed to distance himself from the more radical party policies. And while he struck an upright, sanctimonious pose as premier, he was levelled by accusations that he seduced an eighteen-year-old stenographer in the back seat of a government car after telling her his wife was an invalid and that he was "starved for affection."

Brownlee came to Alberta in the first instance to article as a lawyer. The son of a small-town Ontario general-store owner, he trained as a teacher, taught for two years, and then decided he wanted something more for himself than the life of a village school-master. He enrolled in history and political science courses at the University of Toronto and paid for his tuition and living expenses by selling magazine subscriptions. He graduated with a third-class honours degree in political science.

In 1909, at age twenty-six, Brownlee moved to Calgary. A career in law was just one motivating factor. Another was a desire to renew his relationship with Florence Edy, a twenty-two-year-old arts graduate whom he had met at a skating party in Toronto, and who was studying to be a teacher at Calgary Normal School. Brownlee articled for three years with the Calgary firm of Lougheed and Bennett and was called to the Alberta bar on December 16, 1912. A week later, he and Edy were married in Toronto. They made their home in Calgary's Elboya district, and Brownlee took a job with Muir, Jephson, and Adams, the law firm that did legal work for the United Farmers of Alberta.

In 1915, the Brownlees' first son, John Edy, was born. A second son, Alan Marshall, was born two years later. By that time Florence was ailing with a severe cough, diagnosed as a tubercular infection. In 1919, a daughter was born, only to die shortly afterwards. Florence remained in poor health for the next several years. A full-time maid and Brownlee's sister Maude helped look after her and the boys.

While events at home took a downward turn, Brownlee's professional career flourished. In July 1919, he became the full-time solicitor for the United Grain Growers, a company he helped form through the union of two Alberta grain elevator companies. He also did some work on the side for the United Farmers of Alberta, which was then on the verge of evolving from an economic interest group into a political movement. Through this work, Brownlee became closely acquainted with such leading UFA figures as party president Henry Wise Wood, pioneering socialist William Irvine, farm women's champion Irene Parlby, and future premier Herbert Greenfield.

When the UFA achieved power by defeating the Liberals in 1921, Brownlee was Henry Wise Wood's first choice for premier, although he had not run in the election. The party members preferred Greenfield, a farmer with no real interest in politics. Brownlee was appointed attorney general, and a seat was found for him in the Ponoka constituency. He helped organize the Alberta Wheat Pool in 1923 and took part in prolonged negotiations with Ottawa over the return of Alberta's natural resources. In 1924, he prepared the legislation that ended Prohibition and made the provincial government responsible for the sale, distribution, and taxing of liquor. A year later, in November 1925, Brownlee was the UFA's unanimous choice to take over as premier when Greenfield decided to quit politics. As the power behind the throne, Brownlee had often acted as the main parliamentary spokesman for the government's program because Greenfield—who often claimed to be suffering from laryngitis— didn't like having to deal with the tough questions lobbed at him as premier.

As premier of Alberta, Brownlee became recognized as an important voice for the West, with considerable negotiating skills and a formidable physical presence—he was more than six feet tall, weighed two hundred pounds, and had the bespectacled stare of a giant bald eagle. His skills impressed everyone, including Prime Minister Mackenzie King, who sought advice from the Alberta premier on federal election matters after his Liberal party was defeated in 1930 by R.B. Bennett's Conservatives. One of Brownlee's early achievements as premier was to move the UFA—whose original mandate concerned itself only with the interests of farmers—toward becoming a more traditional, broadly-based political party that served the interests of all citizens.

From 1930 onward, Brownlee was constantly negotiating with Ottawa and with the other western provinces on agricultural and fiscal problems. As the Depression deepened, Alberta bore the brunt of everything that was wrong with the Canadian financial system. Grain and livestock prices fell to levels where the cash return to the farmers would barely cover the costs of shipping products to market. To stem the mounting public criticism of the financial system, Prime Minister Bennett set up a Royal Commission on banking and currency in May 1933 and appointed Brownlee as the only nonbanker to sit on it.

A lawyer's letter initiating the process that eventually led to the premier's downfall arrived in August 1933, just as Brownlee was moving to Ottawa to take his place on the Royal Commission. It began, "We have been instructed to commence action against you for damages for the seduction of Miss Vivian MacMillan." The plaintiff was a Brownlee family friend who worked as a junior stenographer in the provincial attorney general's office. The daughter of former Edson mayor Allan MacMillan, Vivian had first met Brownlee in 1930 when she was a high school student and he was campaigning for the UFA in her hometown. She subsequently moved to Edmonton where, at the invitation of the premier and his wife, she became a frequent visitor to the Brownlee home.

Brownlee reacted to the allegation by trying to phone MacMillan to ask her for an explanation. When she refused to talk to him, he tried phoning her parents, also without success. At that point, he decided to drive to Edson with his wife, Florence, to confront the parents and, in his words, "try to find out what I was being charged with; whether Vivian was pregnant and I was being accused." He found out, a month later, when Neil Maclean, the lawyer for the MacMillans, filed a statement of claim in the Supreme Court of Alberta on behalf of Vivian MacMillan and her father.

Maclean was already acting as counsel in another sex-scandal suit involving a member of the Brownlee government when he took on the MacMillan case. A Liberal party supporter, he had eagerly agreed

Vivian MacMillan on her way to court: "It is peculiar but true."
(GLENBOW ARCHIVES ND-3-6747)

to represent the former wife of UFA public works minister Tony McPherson when she sought to have her divorce annulled on grounds that her husband had tricked her into having an adulterous affair. The case was eventually dismissed, but this did not stop the *Edmonton Bulletin* and other Alberta newspapers from publishing long and detailed accounts of how McPherson and his wife had allegedly entered into a spouse-swapping arrangement with another couple so that each could marry the new partner. The scheme worked out fine for McPherson, who got himself a new wife out of the arrangement. But his ex-wife didn't fare so well. She lost out when her intended decided he wanted to remain single and play the field.

In the Brownlee case, Vivian MacMillan sued for ten thousand dollars and her father sued for five thousand dollars. They laid the seduction charge under the Alberta Seductions Act, a rarely-used statute based on a two-hundred-year-old British law designed to protect female servants from being abused by their male masters. Maclean's statement of claim alleged that Brownlee had become enchanted with MacMillan's "youth and innocence" when he first met her at her parents' home in Edson. He persuaded her to come to Edmonton to take a business course, after which he promised her a government job. Once MacMillan started at business school, he proceeded to seduce her at every opportunity. The trysts occurred, with her silently protesting, two to three times a week over a two-year period, in his car, at his home, and in his office. During one seven-week stretch he "insisted on having connections with her every night he was home."

Brownlee responded by fighting fire with fire. In a counterclaim, he alleged that the MacMillan suit arose from a failure by Vivian MacMillan and her fiancé, John Caldwell, to extort money from him by threatening him with a seduction story that they had invented. Caldwell was a third-year medical student at the University of Alberta, and the counterclaim statement said he was to be paid by "political opponents" for bringing Brownlee's character into disrepute.

The trial opened before Mr. Justice William Ives and a six-man jury on June 25, 1934. Brownlee was represented by M.M. Porter, a

Calgary lawyer who had succeeded him as solicitor for the Alberta Wheat Pool, and by A.L. Smith, a lawyer with a reputation as a skilled cross-examiner. The MacMillans were represented by Maclean and by R.H.C. Harrison. The all-male jury of six included a Stony Plain farmer, a Wainwright poolroom proprietor, and an Edmonton clothier.

Vivian MacMillan took the witness stand on the first day of the trial, and her testimony was reported in such graphic detail in the *Edmonton Bulletin* that Judge Ives interrupted the proceedings to slap contempt charges on publisher Charles Campbell and his reporter, J.S. Cowper. The reporter had characterized Brownlee as a "love-torn, sex-crazed victim of passion and jealousy" after MacMillan said the premier was leading a "lonely, unhappy life." Other newspapers were more restrained. The Calgary *Albertan* told its readers that it would not titillate them with "an orgy of salaciousness" like the Edmonton paper. The *Albertan* would report some details of the case in the interests of "accuracy and fairness" but would "derive no temporary and ephemeral circulation advantage by catering to obscenities and indecency."

And what were the specifics of these alleged "obscenities and indecency"? According to MacMillan, they involved having sex with the premier in various places, including the back seat of his government-issue Studebaker, in his office, and at his home. Her most startling revelation was that she "had connection" with Brownlee in a bedroom that he shared with his younger son, while the son slept next to them in an adjoining twin bed and Brownlee's wife slept in a nearby bedroom. MacMillan testified that Brownlee entreated her to have sex with him because his ailing wife feared another pregnancy would endanger her life. MacMillan said that once she succumbed, she was subjected to a combination of pleas and threats from Brownlee to keep the relationship going. She testified that Brownlee gave her a "pregnancy pill" to prevent conception during the affair.

Under cross-examination, her story began to unravel. A.L. Smith showed that Brownlee was absent from Edmonton on several occasions when she had sworn he was seducing her. These contradictions resulted in one three-month series of daily "connections" being reduced to less than ten days. Asked to explain why Brownlee gave her the contraception pills instead of giving them to his wife, MacMillan replied, "It is peculiar, but true."

No evidence was introduced to corroborate her story. It was her word against his. Brownlee denied her every allegation when he took the stand on June 28, 1934. He testified that at the time when he was allegedly seducing her in the back of his car, he was actually giving an address to the Stettler Chamber of Commerce. At a time when they were supposed to be having sex in his office, he was meeting with the mayor of Raymond. As for her claim that they had sex in his house while the rest of the household was sleeping, Brownlee maintained that his wife was a light sleeper and "the slightest movement around the house wakens her up." Asked to characterize his relationship with Vivian MacMillan, Brownlee said it was "just as near being a member of the family as a person not being a natural son or daughter could be. I would say like a niece."

Before the case went to the jury, Smith surprised the court by withdrawing Brownlee's counterclaim. He gave no explanation for this move, which left some of Brownlee's political enemies suggesting that the counterclaim was nothing more than a bluff. Brownlee's supporters saw the situation differently. They said that the counterclaim became unnecessary when Brownlee's lawyers destroyed MacMillan's evidence.

Judge Ives made it clear in his Saturday afternoon charge to the jury that he was more inclined to believe Brownlee than MacMillan. The story of the female plaintiff, he said, was "wholly and entirely unsupported by any other evidence." There was no evidence of sexual intercourse, and it was "quite clear that the female plaintiff is out and out wrong in her dates."

After four hours and fifty minutes of deliberation, the jury stunned the courtroom by bringing in a guilty verdict, with ten thousand dollars in damages to be paid to MacMillan and five thousand dollars to be paid to her father. The judge was dumbfounded. "I think I should say openly and publicly, while you are present, that I strongly disagree with your answers," he told the jury. "The evidence does not warrant them." He refused to enter a judgment and adjourned court for the weekend. But Brownlee didn't wait around for the Monday morning judgment. The verdict had turned him from upright premier into scoundrel politician. He resigned immediately as leader of the United Farmers of Alberta and as premier. Richard Gavin Reid, the dour Scottish-born minister of natural resources, replaced him.

On July 2, 1934, Judge Ives delivered his formal judgment, dismissing the MacMillan action with costs charged to the plaintiffs. The decision set off an unprecedented spate of editorials in newspapers across the country, criticizing the judge for his attack on the sanctity of jury verdicts. The *Calgary Herald* noted that the province of Alberta had already suffered a considerable amount of unfavourable publicity over the case. "It looks as if more of the same thing will have to be suffered before *finis* is written to it."

The *Herald's* prediction proved correct. On September 19, 1934, the MacMillans launched an appeal against the Ives judgment. It was heard in the Appellate Division of the Alberta Supreme Court in mid-January 1935, and a three-to-two decision dismissing the appeal was handed down on February 2. Chief Justice Harvey, who wrote the majority report, was scathing in his criticism of Vivian MacMillan's testimony. "Her whole story is of an impossible, not to say incredible, character," he said, noting that, in every other seduction case to appear before the courts, "there was a birth or pregnancy to prove sexual intercourse."

Between the Brownlee trial and the Appeal Court verdict, the Alberta political scene was in turmoil. While the Liberals hoped to take advantage of voter disenchantment with the UFA in the wake of the McPherson and Brownlee scandals, they were discredited by accusations made public when Brownlee filed his later-withdrawn counterclaim against the MacMillans. The counterclaim alleged a conspiracy between MacMillan's fiancé and Brownlee's "political opponents," and those opponents were widely believed to be the Liberals. Adding to the Liberals' woes was the fact that a new political party called Social Credit was coming on strong under the leadership of a school principal and radio evangelist named William "Bible Bill" Aberhart.

The Social Credit party won power in August 1935, annihilating both the ruling UFA and the opposition Liberals, who lost eight of the thirteen seats they had held at dissolution. Brownlee lost his Ponoka seat to a political neophyte named Edith Rogers, and McPherson lost his seat in Little Bow. Brownlee retired from politics and returned to practising law. The United Grain Growers reappointed him as their solicitor, which suggested that the details of his withdrawn counterclaim had gained widespread circulation and that the farmers were inclined to believe his allegation that he had been brought down by his political enemies.

The lawyers for Vivian MacMillan continued to press her case in the courts. On March 1, 1937, almost three years after the original verdict, she was finally vindicated. The Supreme Court of Canada overturned the Alberta Court of Appeal decision and restored the verdict of the trial jury. It rejected the argument of the Alberta court that a birth or pregnancy had to occur to prove sexual intercourse and awarded MacMillan ten thousand dollars. Brownlee paid the damages, plus the costs of all trials. He then decided to launch his own appeal, which he did to the Judicial Committee of the Privy Council in Britain. His English lawyer argued that to "give a woman damages for the voluntary loss of her chastity" was a "radical departure" from English law. But the Privy Council confirmed the judgment of the Supreme Court of Canada.

Despite his legal problems, Brownlee had no difficulty rebuilding his career. In 1942, he was elected to the board of directors of the United Grain Growers, and he also served on the boards of various food service companies. Six years later he was named president and general manager of United Grain Growers, and he maintained offices and homes in both Calgary and Winnipeg.

In Calgary, Brownlee lived just a few blocks away from where Vivian MacMillan worked as a construction company secretary and bookkeeper. She never married the medical student named in the withdrawn Brownlee counterclaim. Instead, she returned to Edson and married Henry Sorensen, the owner of a local ice cream parlour. They separated and divorced during the Second World War. MacMillan moved to Calgary with her young son, Allan, and began working for construction company owner Frank Howie. She eventually married Howie and lived with him in various comfortable Calgary homes that they bought or built themselves.

Brownlee continued to serve as president of United Grain Growers until two weeks before his death. He streamlined the company's financial structure and made the grain elevator system more efficient by closing small operations and concentrating on larger delivery points. He died on July 15, 1961, at age seventy-seven.

MacMillan moved to British Columbia's Okanagan Valley in the late 1960s, after she was stricken with a severe case of emphysema. She then lived in Arizona for about ten years before settling in Fort Lauderdale, Florida. She was sixty-eight when she died in Florida on August 1, 1980.

She seems to have put the Brownlee affair firmly behind her when she moved back to Edson after the trial. So firmly, in fact, that she never told her son Allan about it. He didn't find out his mother's role in the scandal until 1996, when he came up from Florida to visit relatives in Edson.

Postscript

To prevent a repeat of the damaging newspaper coverage that plagued both the Brownlee affair and the wife-swapping case involving Tony McPherson, the UFA government passed a law in 1935, shortly before losing power to the Socreds, that restricted what could be printed in the papers about civil court cases. Unique in Canada, the Alberta Judicature Act prohibited publishing anything but basic details of a civil proceeding prior to a trial or judgment. The law remained on the books for more than fifty years. The *Edmonton Journal* challenged the law in 1985 as an unconstitutional violation of freedom of the press, but it lost the case at the Alberta Court of Queen's Bench. Four years later, the Supreme Court of Canada ruled unanimously that the Alberta law was unconstitutional and struck it from the books. The rarely used Alberta Seductions Act, meanwhile, was finally repealed by the provincial government in 1984.

Guy Weadick

Cowboy showman

1885–1953

~

Florence LaDue

Trick roper

1883–1951

Calgary was turning away from its ranching and farming roots and looking toward a bright future as a commercial and industrial centre in 1912 when a gregarious vaudeville entertainer named Guy Weadick came to town to organize the first Calgary Stampede. The city's annual exhibition had become an industrial show featuring automotive exhibits and aviation displays, so Weadick's Stampede was seen as a one-time salute to Calgary's frontier past. It ended up becoming something much more permanent.

It took several years for the Stampede to become an annual event. The 1912 Stampede, though a crowd-pleaser, was an organizational disaster due to the twenty-seven-year-old Weadick's lack of managerial experience. As a performer, he knew how to put on a good show, but he didn't know yet how to run a smooth rodeo operation. It wasn't until 1923, when the exhibition and the Stampede were formally combined, that cautious Calgarians agreed to give Weadick an opportunity to manage the Stampede as an annual affair.

Born in Rochester, New York, Weadick was drawn to the cowboy life as a teenager, inspired by the stories he heard from uncles who worked as ranch hands in Wyoming and California. As he travelled from the Dakotas to Montana, Weadick learned about horses

Publicity shot of Guy Weadick and Florence LaDue:
"The Calgary Stampede will make Buffalo Bill's Wild West
extravaganza look like a sideshow."
(GLENBOW ARCHIVES NA-3164-70)

and riding and roping, and he saw that the essential skills used by ranch hands in the course of their daily work could also become marketable commodities in the entertainment world. In 1904, he made his first visit to Alberta and saw some impressive performances at a riding and roping competition in Cardston. A year later he was touring the rodeo circuit himself as a trick roper, teamed with a black cowboy named Bill Pickett, whose specialty was an early form of steer wrestling known as bulldogging. It involved Pickett leaping from his horse, grabbing a steer by the horns, wrestling it to the ground, and biting the steer's upper lip. It was a spectacular feat and audiences loved it.

In 1906, Weadick said goodbye to Pickett, and Florence LaDue became his new partner, both in business and in life. She was a lawyer's daughter from Minnesota who learned to ride and rope on her father's ranch and ran away from home when he refused to let her join a Wild West show. She met Weadick when both landed jobs with the Colonel Fred T. Cummins Wild West and Indian Congress, and they married five weeks later.

Weadick and LaDue spent two years with the Cummins show, perfecting their trick roping and fancy roping act. In 1908, they joined the Miller Brothers' 101 Ranch Wild West show, one of the more successful of the travelling Buffalo Bill show imitators. One of their first stops was in Calgary, where the twenty-three-year-old Weadick had the gumption to approach H.C. McMullen, the livestock agent for the Canadian Pacific Railway, and propose that together they organize a week-long rodeo for the city. McMullen didn't think the time was right for such a promotion, but he promised to contact Weadick whenever the idea seemed feasible.

Weadick and LaDue spent the next four years on the international vaudeville circuit, performing in the Broadway show *Billy the Kid* and touring Europe. Weadick landed in trouble in Paris when he told an audience that he had been swindled by a barber who overcharged him for a shave and haircut. The barber, said Weadick, was "a worse robber than any of the bandits of the Old West." The men in the audience were not impressed. They challenged Weadick to a duel and were even less impressed when he offered his choice of weapon as the lariat. The duel was called off and Weadick and

LaDue left France in a hurry. They were running out of money when a letter arrived from McMullen inviting Weadick to come back to Calgary and discuss his rodeo proposal.

Calgary's population had doubled to fifty thousand during the four years Weadick and LaDue were on the road, and small one-day rodeos had become popular in nearby cattle country. CPR agent McMullen thought a big rodeo in Calgary might now be a popular draw and that Weadick, with his international rodeo connections, would make it a success.

It was a tough sell. The exhibition board didn't want to sponsor a rodeo, and there was little support money available from Calgary businessmen. Alberta was looking ahead, they said, and ranching was a thing of the past. McMullen and Weadick were at the point of abandoning the project when four wealthy cattlemen stepped forward and agreed to bankroll the rodeo to the tune of one hundred thousand dollars. Weadick assured the four—Pat Burns, George Lane, Archie McLean, and A.E. Cross—that they would not be disappointed. The event, he said, would "make Buffalo Bill's Wild West extravaganza look like a sideshow."

Weadick chose the name "stampede" to separate the Calgary event from other rodeos and, as a promotional venture, it was undoubtedly a success. Though poorly organized, it drew more than forty thousand people to Calgary during its six-day run in September 1912, and it earned enough money to pay back the investment to the four backers. But the Big Four, as they were called, weren't ready to finance a repeat event the next year, and nobody else in Calgary was willing to put up the money either. Weadick moved on to Winnipeg, where he staged what he billed as "Canada's second annual world's greatest" rodeo in 1913, and then he and LaDue rejoined the 101 Ranch Wild West show as trick ropers. But Weadick was now more interested in promoting shows than in performing in them. In 1914, he did the publicity for a 101 Ranch show that had a successful six-month run in London, and in 1916 he took on his biggest challenge yet when he organized New York's first professional rodeo. It was a flop, but Weadick was learning from his mistakes.

By 1919, Calgary was ready to give the Stampede a second try. The First World War was over, and the city went all out to celebrate peace in Europe. The Big Four reassembled to finance the Calgary Victory Stampede, and once again Weadick was the man in charge.

Weadick ran the Victory Stampede more efficiently than he had the 1912 event, but attendance fell far short of expectations. Calgary still was not ready to commit to an annual event. Weadick and LaDue, however, were ready to make a commitment to Calgary. They had found a ranch property south of the city near Longview, and from 1920 onward it became their home. They named it Stampede Ranch and operated it as a guest ranch, with roping and branding events, and chuckwagon and trail rides offered as featured attractions. "Come where there are no snakes nor poisonous insects," said the brochure. "Explore virgin valleys which have never been explored by tourists."

LaDue looked after the business affairs of the ranch, and she was said to be a hard taskmaster. She treated the horses better than she treated the hired hands, who were expected to work long hours for low pay. Weadick handled the promotions for the ranch, which was a role that suited him well because he was, in the words of historian James Gray, a "two-fisted drinking man ... an unreconstructable hedonist who took his fun where he found it." He and LaDue ran the ranch during the spring and summer and returned to the vaudeville circuit in winter.

In the spring of 1923, Weadick finally received a long-awaited invitation. Attendance at the Calgary exhibition had been declining, and the directors wondered if Weadick would revive the Stampede once again, only now to be held as an annual event in conjunction with the exhibition. Weadick agreed, but he drove a hard bargain. He would do it, he said, on a six-month contract for five thousand dollars. That was more than the mayor of Calgary was earning at the time, but the directors decided to take the risk.

The gamble paid off. Weadick worked hard for his money and the 1923 Stampede was a success. So were the Stampedes that followed. Attendance rose steadily from 137,838 in 1923 to 258,469 in 1929. Then came an attendance drop, followed by a deficit and a decision by the exhibition board to cut the budget. Weadick wanted the 1932 Stampede to be a magnificent twentieth-anniversary celebration of the event he had created for Calgary, but the Depression had hit Calgary hard and the directors resented Weadick's freewheeling attitude toward money. Disgusted, Weadick got excessively drunk before the closing ceremonies and shouted at the crowd, "I put on your first Stampede and I've just put on your last." A month later, the exhibition board fired him.

Weadick sued for wrongful dismissal, which the board defended by saying his heavy drinking prevented him from doing an effective job. The judge sided with Weadick, ruling that drinking was part of his job as Stampede promoter, and awarded him six months' salary plus seventeen hundred dollars in legal costs. But the win didn't mean Weadick was reinstated. The board had eliminated the position of Stampede manager and was now organizing the rodeo from the main office of the exhibition.

Weadick and LaDue struggled through the rest of the 1930s and into the 1940s. The death of vaudeville put an end to their performing careers, and they were never able to make much money from their guest ranch. "Income tax doesn't bother me, as I have no income," said Weadick bitterly. In 1947, the couple sold the ranch and bought a home in High River. Weadick wrote articles for the *High River Times* and did public relations for the High River rodeo while LaDue became active in community affairs.

In August 1951, LaDue suffered a heart attack and died. "A true partner" was the inscription Weadick put on her grave marker. Theirs had been a sometimes rocky relationship because Weadick often cheated on her and LaDue invariably found out about it. Friends could always tell, from the new items of furniture around the house, whenever he was trying to seek forgiveness from his strong-willed wife. After one spat, LaDue refused to ride in Weadick's car for several months because she had seen him escorting another woman in the vehicle. But theirs was as much a partnership as a marriage and on that basis it worked.

Weadick married a family friend named Dolly Mott about eight months after LaDue died. Three months after that, in July 1952, he was invited to be a guest of honour at the Calgary Stampede. The reconciliation, on the fortieth anniversary of his first Stampede, came just in time. Weadick died the next year at age sixty-eight. Some said he never really recovered from LaDue's death and that his marriage to Dolly was not a happy one. The Stampede board showed it no longer held a grudge by naming a rodeo trophy after him and installing a bronze memorial tablet in his name in the building that is named after the four wealthy cattlemen who bankrolled the first Stampede.

Robert "Streetcar" Brown Sr.
Wildcatter

1886–1948

~

Robert "Bobby" Brown Jr.
Wildcatter

1914–1972

They were the most formidable father-and-son team in the history of Canadian wildcat exploration drilling, two hard-drinking gamblers who built fortunes on hunches. Robert "Streetcar" Brown—his nickname came from the fact that he once ran the Calgary street railway system—became the biggest operator in the oil patch in 1936 when he struck oil in Turner Valley. Son Bobby became a big operator himself in the 1950s when he expanded the company his father had founded into Canada's largest independent oil producer.

Brown Sr. worked for the City of Calgary for twenty-five years before he made his big oil strike in 1936. Born in Point Levis, Quebec, the son of an immigrant Irish electrician, he followed his father into the trade at age fourteen. He worked for the General Electric Company in Schenectady, New York, as a lab assistant to Charles Steinmetz, the German-born American scientist who pioneered in many fields of electrical research.

An accomplished electrical engineer who studied hard to become a leader in his field, Brown came to Calgary in 1906 after being hired—at age twenty—as superintendent of the Northwest Electric Company. He left after a year to supervise construction of a hydro plant in Nelson, British Columbia, and returned in 1911 as head of

Calgary's municipal electric light department. A few years later, he was put in charge of the city's streetcar system as well.

Shortly after Brown's return to Calgary, a vibrant new industry was born in the grain fields and cattle country of southern Alberta. In May 1914, a flow of liquefied petroleum gas gushed from a Turner Valley well drilled by an Ontario-born entrepreneur named Archie Dingman. The burly figure of Brown can be seen as a spectator in the photograph taken to mark the occasion. Son Bobby would have been two months old at the time.

Brown was either very efficient or not very busy in his role as a municipal boss because he had lots of time to dabble in extracurricular activities. With the apparent blessing of the city fathers, he set up a network of small electrical utility companies in the towns east of Calgary and invested the proceeds in oil shares. Actively interested in the emerging oil business, which he studied with the same enthusiasm he once brought to mastering the technical complexities of electricity, Brown promoted the theory that a substantial pool of crude oil must lie beneath the natural gas fields of Turner Valley. People in the industry disagreed with him, but Brown was prepared to back his hunch with money if he could find others willing to join him.

In 1934, Brown found a partner in George Bell, who was proprietor of the Calgary *Albertan* newspaper. They leased sixty acres of land in Turner Valley where they hoped they might find oil and looked for money to finance the drilling of a single wildcat (i.e., speculative) well. Finding money was difficult in the middle of the Depression, however, so Brown and Bell had to adopt a new method of financing. They formed a company, Turner Valley Royalties, and instead of offering variable-yield shares to investors, they promised a fixed, royalty-like percentage of the income earned by the well if it proved successful. (If the well was unsuccessful, the investors would receive nothing more than their original stake.) Seventy percent of a well's earnings were subject to the payment of royalties, which meant that potential returns to the investors could be high if the well was prolific.

It took Brown more than two years to secure the necessary financial backing. He mortgaged his house and car and borrowed on his

Oilpatch pioneer R. A. Brown and son Bobby:
"I find the money and they find the oil."
(GLENBOW ARCHIVES NA-2335-3)

insurance policies and still had to suspend drilling several times due to lack of money. But he continued to promote the project and finally, in June 1936, his persistence paid off. A burst of crude oil soared upwards from the well, and the second important era in Alberta's oil industry began. The Turner Valley discovery remained the biggest find in Canada—some said the biggest in the British Commonwealth—until the Leduc strike eleven years later. The investors in Turner Valley Royalties began to see profits within a few months.

Bobby Brown was twenty-one and studying commerce at the University of Alberta when the Turner Valley well came in as a gusher, splattering oil onto the surrounding field. In some histories of the period, he is said to have asked his father, "What does it mean, Dad?" and that his father replied, "It means we get out of debt, son." But given that the younger Brown had always heard his father talking about oil, it seems reasonable to conclude that the story is part of the mythology that has accumulated about the petroleum industry in western Canada.

Brown Sr., who was then fifty, quit his two jobs with the city and son Bobby dropped out of university to work full-time with his father. Bobby's accountancy professor warned him it might be a rash move. "Don't worry, professor," Bobby told him. "I'm going to hire your best two students to work for me." And eventually he did. Two of Bobby's former classmates provided him with senior accounting support during the 1940s.

Within a year of the Turner Valley discovery, father and son controlled a string of one-well operations, which they drilled on leased properties close to their original strike and financed by selling royalty interests. Each well was owned by a different Brown company—with a name such as B. & B. Royalties, Three Point Petroleum, or Royal Crest Petroleum—and was designed to attract small investors. "We raise money from anyone we can talk into investing a thousand dollars," said Bobby. It was his first attempt at attracting investment capital, and he proved to be good at it. If a well was successful, the company stayed in business. If it ran dry, the company folded.

By 1938, the father-and-son treasure seekers had so many companies and so many wells—more than thirty of them at one point—

that keeping track of the paperwork proved to be a headache. To streamline the operation, they set up an umbrella company, Brown Consolidated Petroleums, to keep all the purchasing, leasing, and administrative activity under one roof.

Another problem that surfaced during this period was Brown Sr.'s drinking. Every so often he would move into a hotel room with a large quantity of liquor and remain there—usually for several days—until the last bottle was drained. Bobby would fill in for him during these binges and try to put a brave face on things. But the absences caused pain to the family and eventually affected Brown Sr.'s health. He suffered from heart problems and pernicious anemia.

In 1939, with investment capital in Canada drying up, father and son travelled to London in search of money. They returned with only eighty thousand dollars, but made it appear as if they had acquired more. They told reporters that the money would allow them to drill three new wells and that one would be Bobby's first solo wildcat venture. Bobby was determined to make his own reputation in the oil business and not be seen just as Brown Sr.'s up-and-coming youngster.

Nothing came of Bobby's first venture, in the Jumping Pound area west of Calgary. Nor did anything come of his subsequent ventures, in the Priddis area southwest of the city. But Bobby did earn the respect of his peers as a committed wildcatter. He sold the Jumping Pound lease to Shell Oil in 1942 and negotiated a royalty interest for himself that paid off eventually when Shell struck what became a major gas field.

In 1943, Bobby joined the navy and was posted to Ottawa as an oil procurement officer. He took a suite in the Chateau Laurier hotel and entertained lavishly. This marked the beginning of a drinking problem that would eventually prove more destructive to him than it did to his father.

When he returned to Calgary, Bobby decided that the oil business in Alberta had reached a dead end. All of the wildcatting activity, including his own, had failed to find the new oil field needed to replace the dwindling resources of Turner Valley. He borrowed one hundred thousand dollars from his father and set up three companies to import home appliances from the United States. That venture turned sour in 1947 when the Canadian government, worried about the balance of trade, placed an embargo on such imports. To pay off his debts, Bobby returned to the business he knew best. Imperial Oil's discovery at Leduc had rekindled exploration fever in western Canada, and Bobby was soon back in the oil business.

Brown Sr. died of a heart attack at age sixty-two in May 1948. That left Bobby firmly in control of the family company, which was now named Federated Petroleums. He expanded rapidly, borrowing money in increasingly large amounts. When he received $8 million to acquire Imperial's Turner Valley interests in 1949, it was the largest oil loan ever made by a Canadian bank to that time. And when he gained control of Home Oil in 1951 by secretly buying its shares on the open market, Brown Jr. was on his way to becoming the biggest independent operator in the oil patch. "I have an effective arrangement with my managers," he said. "I find the money and they find the oil."

Brown merged Federated with Home in 1955, and under his leadership Home became one of the most successful wildcatters in Canada. Its biggest strike was an oil field discovered near Swan Hills in 1957 that proved to be the largest in Canada at that time. Brown's tendency to walk the financial tightrope in pursuit of bigger and bigger oil patch scores made him a legend in the world of Canadian business. But his recklessness, compounded by his deepening alcoholism, worried conservative Home Oil investors. They felt that one of his gambles might one day blow the whole game.

In 1959, Brown committed a major tactical error when he tried to gain control of the giant TransCanada PipeLines. It was an expensive blunder that cost Home more than $8 million when TransCanada share prices dropped. By 1960, Home was $52 million in debt. Yet far from demonstrating fiscal prudence, Brown persisted in playing the role of the flamboyant tycoon, spending $1.3 million on a Grumman Gulfstream, the most luxurious executive aircraft available, and entertaining regally on both sides of the Atlantic.

Brown eventually recovered from the TransCanada fiasco when he guided Home to a successful gas exploration venture in the North Sea off the coast of England. But money problems plagued him again in 1970 when he gambled more than $70 million of his own and

Home's money to become involved in what seemed like a potentially lucrative play, on Alaska's North Slope. The potential proved unfounded, and when the loss figures were tallied Brown found himself facing bankruptcy. His personal debt stood at a staggering $26 million. To add to his travails, he suffered two mild heart attacks followed by a slight stroke. A note he scrawled on his desk pad said, "A lot of kidney damage; outlook one or two years."

Brown tried to sell Home to Ashland Oil of Kentucky, but the federal government blocked the deal, saying there was "political sensitivity" about a sale to an American company. Instead, Brown reluctantly surrendered control of the company to Consumers' Gas of Toronto, a move that didn't please him but did allow him to escape bankruptcy. Eight months later, on January 3, 1972, Brown died of a heart attack at age fifty-seven.

Thus ended the era of one dominating individual exerting strong personal control over the operations of a big energy company. Like his father before him, Bobby Brown Jr. ran his business as his own personal fiefdom and saw it grow into a multimillion-dollar operation. But he was the last of a breed. Henceforth, professional management teams would run the major energy companies, with checks and balances in place to ensure that the gambles were not too risky. *Oilweek* magazine reporter Les Rowland wrote the obituary that best summed up Bobby Brown's high-flying way of doing business. "We can only imagine that Bobby is still scanning the scene here from his next incarnation," wrote Rowland. "But it's possible he may be too busy making a deal on the golden pavements."

Fred Speed

Mayoralty candidate

1891–1975

Fred Speed was one of the most consistent losers in Edmonton's political history. Starting in 1934, he ran seven times for the mayor's chair and finished each time at the bottom of the polls. He also ran unsuccessfully for alderman on three occasions, and would have run for school board except that he missed the deadline for filing nomination papers. Yet despite his long string of failures, he invariably attracted more press coverage than some of the winning candidates.

Speed's efforts to enter Edmonton politics began about twenty-five years after he came to Canada from England in 1910. Born in Woodford, Essex, Speed decided as a teenager that England was too dull for him, and he often talked of immigrating to Canada when he was strolling through Epping Forest with his girlfriend, Amy. She said she would be happy to accompany him to Canada after they were married. He trained as a carpenter, saved his money, married Amy, and set sail for the land of his dreams.

He worked as an independent contractor after he arrived in Edmonton, building houses and renting them. When he took his first run at the mayor's chair in 1934, he said he was tired of "quack" politics. That effort resulted in fifty votes. The next year he campaigned for monetary reform. "The Bank Act of Canada is a fraud," said Speed, echoing the sentiments of William Aberhart, whose Social Credit party won the provincial election that year. "The new council should make an effort to show the way for discarding the money system in favour of a production system," said Speed. He also campaigned for replacing city streetcars with buses. "We should take the tracks and cars and throw them in the river," he said. He received seventy-four votes. A pattern was emerging. Mainstream voter support was clearly beyond his grasp.

In 1936, Speed lost ground at the polls, receiving only fifty-four votes after alleging that a rival candidate was "so crooked that he'd steal the front steps off the civic block." But, offered Speed, "I'll put them back again." That was about the only comment in his own words that Speed uttered during the 1936 campaign. The rest of his speeches came from the collected works of Shakespeare. "The plays of Shakespeare are my manifesto," he said. "The answers to the problems facing the city of Edmonton can be found in the great dramas." To prove his point, at an all-candidates' meeting he recited several speeches from *Henry the Fifth* and—without saying what relevancy it might have to civic politics—the final death scene from *Hamlet*. He also offered to throw in some scenes from *The Merchant of Venice* but the other mayoralty candidates objected.

Speed abandoned Shakespeare in 1937 and campaigned on a platform of appropriating the Macdonald Hotel from its Canadian National Railways owners and making it the new city hall. He also campaigned for better conditions for Edmonton's birds: "Let us with a full heart deal kindly with Our Lord's helpless little feathered creatures in a manner bespeaking our decency and compassion as human beings. Remember, a vote for Frederick J. Speed is a vote for more and better civic bird baths in Edmonton." He received sixty-two votes. Undeterred, Speed announced he would be back the next year with a new platform. "All they have to do is eliminate the direct vote and change over to proportional representation based on the popular vote," he said. "Then I'm in." As part of his new platform he planned to give the city "more and better public downtown comfort stations."

As it turned out, 1938 was Speed's best year yet at the polls. One hundred and ninety-eight citizens rewarded his persistence, if not his performance, with their votes. But he still remained firmly in last place. Winner John Fry polled more than thirteen thousand votes.

Speed left Edmonton in 1939 and moved to Victoria, where he didn't have anything to do with municipal politics. But in a letter to Mayor Fry, he warned that he would be back. "There was not any Speed in the election this year or last," he wrote. "And that accounts for many things." Things in Edmonton would never start to improve, he said, until Fred Speed was in the mayor's chair.

Speed returned to Edmonton in 1943 and was once again in the news, but not now because he was running for mayor. He made the headlines after he tried to read the Bible at an Edmonton public school. "It will be even better than Shakespeare," he assured the principal. The principal referred the matter to the school board, which turned down Speed's request. Outraged, Speed announced his intention to stand as a candidate in the school board elections. Unfortunately, he arrived at city hall just minutes after the deadline for nominations had passed, and two election officials refused to admit his candidacy. "Here I stand," said Speed melodramatically, "a rose caught between two thorns."

In 1945, Speed attempted to make his sixth bid for the mayor's chair, but once again he failed to comply with nomination requirements. This time the city clerk refused to accept his candidacy because Speed had registered his home in his wife's name and thus lacked the necessary property ownership qualifications. Speed protested but to no avail. The clerk's decision stood and Speed's name did not appear on the ballot.

Speed resolved his property ownership problem and tried a different strategy in the 1947 election, running simultaneously for mayor and alderman. His long-suffering wife also ran, against her will, for the school board. Neither came close. Speed actually did better than expected, polling 1,554 votes in the two-man mayoralty race. But that was still far short of the seventeen thousand votes received by the winner, Harry Ainlay. Council later amended the law so that a candidate could only run for one office at a time.

In 1948, Speed ran for alderman only and received 928 votes. The following year he made another bid for mayor, denouncing his opponents in the process. "This is the seventh time I have run for mayor of Edmonton, and this time I mean it," he said. "I don't see any opposition, just a bunch of deadwood. This deadwood has been hanging around city hall for too many years. Edmonton is not worth a hill of beans when we have dummies like these in control. We should turn the whole bunch out and put in a man who knows what he is doing. I stand for service, personality, efficiency, and duty. But don't vote for me. Vote for the others and get what you deserve." More than twenty-six thousand voters got what presumably they deserved. Speed received 289 votes.

Speed lowered his sights in 1950 to run as alderman, with the usual poor result. Sick throughout most of the campaign, Speed had his wife appear for him at public meetings. The next year, Speed went to England on vacation and impressed a reporter for London's *Daily Mail* with his stories about life in Canada. The reporter characterized Speed as a "typical Canadian" with a "natural Canadian drawl" and said he was known in Edmonton as a "philosopher, poet, writer, actor, astronomer, logician, and spiritual philanthropist." The *Mail* claimed he had published "hundreds of philosophical articles, and his voice is well known on Canadian radio." Describing Speed's adventures in politics, the *Mail* said, "just a handful of votes has kept him from office each year" and suggested it might be because Speed had never taken out Canadian citizenship. "I'm British born and British I shall stay," the perennial candidate was quoted as saying.

Speed didn't make it back to Edmonton in time for the 1951 mayoralty race. He wrote to council saying he was tied up in London participating in a public debate on "The Car Owner versus the Pedestrian." William Hawrelak won the election by acclamation that year and Speed announced he would challenge him in 1952, apparently unaware that the city was now electing its mayors to two-year terms. When Hawrelak stood for re-election in 1953, however, Speed's name was not on the ballot. He did go to city hall to file nomination papers but changed his mind at the last minute.

That was the last time the seven-time mayoralty candidate considered running for election. "The deadline for nominations passed at twelve noon today and there was no word from Fred Speed," local historian Tony Cashman told his Edmonton radio audience in September 1955, just before Hawrelak was re-elected by acclamation for the second time. Speed had returned to Victoria, where he died in February 1975 at age eighty-four. "He made Edmonton a more interesting place to live," said Cashman.

Harold "Goofy" McMasters

Boxer

1895–1951

Harold McMasters used many nicknames during his spectacularly unsuccessful career as a professional boxer in Alberta: the Battler, the Alberta Assassin, the Unknown Undertaker, Heartless Harold. As a wrestler he used the nickname, the Edmonton Bonecrusher. But the one that suited him best was Goofy. This amiable loser became identified with public silliness and failure long before such professional underdogs as Eddie "the Eagle" Edwards (the Olympic ski jumper) and the Jamaican Olympic bobsled team turned defeat into an art form.

McMasters came to Alberta from Peterborough, Ontario, in 1919 and over the next twenty years he lost ninety-six times in the ring. A big, lumbering heavyweight with the strength of six ordinary men, he made his boxing debut at Edmonton's Empire Theatre and lost the match without throwing a punch. He tried to enter the ring by leaping over the ropes, caught his foot in a turnbuckle, and plunged headfirst into a water bucket, knocking himself out cold. That became the pattern for all his subsequent fights. Goofy didn't just lose his bouts, he bombed in dramatic fashion. He established criteria for failure that will never be challenged. "He was the worst," said Edmonton historian Tony Cashman. "And yet he managed to be the worst with such abiding integrity, such earnest dedication, and such overriding dignity of spirit, that he is remembered not only with affection but admiration."

Audiences from Fairview to Brooks paid to see Goofy lose, and he never disappointed them. In Brooks, he scored the only knockout of his career but it was against a spectator, not an opponent. Pitted against a formidable heavyweight named Dan O'Dowd, who once went eight rounds with world champion Gene Tunney, Goofy first tried to throw the match by dropping to the canvas and feigning unconsciousness. When the referee warned him he would forfeit his share of the purse unless he got up and fought, Goofy charged across the ring with fists flailing. O'Dowd stepped aside, and Goofy went through the ropes, landed in the fourth row, and knocked out a police magistrate.

Everywhere he boxed, he became the talk of the town. In Stettler he tried fighting with his back turned until the referee intervened and forced him to face his opponent. In Ponoka he ended a match before it began when he accidentally pulled a corner post out of its moorings and caused the entire ring to collapse. In Peace River he persuaded a stronger opponent to prolong the action by fighting with his arms taped to his side. That unorthodox arrangement lasted only until Goofy landed a low blow. The opponent lost his temper, burst his restraints, and abruptly ended the fight.

Goofy's flair for getting media attention ensured a big turnout whenever he fought. He promoted the Peace River match by having himself photographed next to a huge leaning tree, pretending to straighten it. He persuaded sportscaster Bill Adams to feature him on the first fight card ever broadcast in Alberta; it was aired live by Calgary's CJOC radio station in 1929. And when the Pathé News people paid him twenty-five cents to appear in one of their newsreels, Goofy was so proud of the attention that he refused to cash the cheque.

Away from the ring, Goofy made a living carrying advertising sandwich boards for Edmonton merchants and promoting the programs at city movie houses. He carried his signs up and down Jasper Avenue and skated around the arena with them between periods at the hockey games. "He skated in a manner that no one who works at being comical could ever hope to imitate," said historian Cashman. If the event called for a costume, Goofy was happy to oblige. He did a promotion for a coal company by dressing as a devil, complete with horns and tail, and chasing a friend down Jasper Avenue with a pitchfork. He advertised a plumbing company in the middle of winter by stripping down to his boxer shorts and sitting outside in a bathtub blowing bubbles. To plug the 1932 Eddie Cantor movie, *The Kid from Spain*, Goofy dressed as a bullfighter and paraded through the downtown leading a reluctant cow. The cow sat down in the middle of the street, and Goofy's futile efforts to move the animal made for better entertainment than the movie they were promoting.

He never worked at the same job for long. He ran a shoeshine stall opposite the St. Regis Hotel for a few months but lost the concession when he began spending more time in the beer parlour than he did shining shoes. He worked intermittently as a furniture mover and as a bouncer, and was once hired to sit in the window of a cigar store dressed in Native regalia. The store offered a free box of cigars to anyone who could make the "Indian" smile. Goofy could never keep a straight face so it was only a matter of time before he lost that job too.

During the 1930s, Goofy went into the military, training with the Nineteenth Alberta Dragoons at Sarcee Camp on the southwest outskirts of Calgary and volunteering for overseas service as a rifleman with the Loyal Edmonton Regiment in 1939. He hoped to see some action in Sicily, but the generals must have known about his losing record as a boxer because they kept him in England for the duration of the war. They put him in charge of the regimental barracks and encouraged him to entertain the troops with a wrestling act. Goofy worked on the act with an Edmonton wrestler named Steve Jostle. The two developed such an effective show that when they put on a wrestling demonstration on a baronial estate in Hampshire, the local farmhands were so shocked by the display of violence that they asked the lord of the manor to step in and stop the slaughter.

Goofy spent time in London during the Blitz and was twice reported missing and believed killed in the air raids. When he returned to barracks, military doctors discovered that he had a heart problem and ordered him to stay out of the ring for the sake of his health. But Goofy couldn't resist the call of the ring. He continued wrestling in England until the end of the war.

Goofy moved into the Salvation Army hostel after he returned to Edmonton and lived there for the rest of his life. He continued to shine shoes and do other odd jobs, spending the proceeds at the St. Regis Hotel beer parlour. His ailing heart finally gave out in December 1951 after he had spent the day working at a carnival and the evening eating half a bucket of dill pickles that had been left over at a hamburger concession. He was buried with full military honours after a service conducted by the Salvation Army. "He always gave the best he had," said historian Cashman. "His best wasn't very good, although he never knew it and it never got him anywhere. But he still kept on giving it with earnest determination."

John James Maloney

Ku Klux Klan leader

1897–1963

In 1932, the province of Alberta became the first and to date the only jurisdiction in the British Commonwealth to grant an incorporation charter to the Ku Klux Klan. At a time when American states were systematically banning the secret society and Klan membership was declining throughout the United States, the organization found new and fertile ground to till in Alberta. This province gave the Klan a charter that made its activities legal, even though one of its stated goals was "racial purity."

How could the Klan—which, at its height, boasted a membership of seven thousand in Alberta—acquire a charter legitimizing its racist and intolerant attitudes in a province where wholesome living and Bible reading were viewed as admirable frontier-bred traits? One reason was the dominance in Alberta during that time of the Orange Order, an imperialistic Protestant organization that shared some of the white supremacist beliefs of the Klan. Another was the persuasive character and charismatic appeal of a xenophobic ex-Catholic dissident named John James Maloney.

Maloney, born in Hamilton, Ontario, to immigrant Irish-Catholic parents, was a former candidate for the Roman Catholic priesthood who left a Montreal seminary after deciding he was not prepared to take the required vow of celibacy. "Nature, for a definite reason, gave us certain passions," he said. "For any man or set of men to make laws contrary to this is not only immoral but absurd as well."

In 1919, after recovering in a Montreal convent from the effects of the 1918 flu epidemic, Maloney became a subscription agent in Hamilton for the *Catholic Register* newspaper. He kept the job for eighteen months but lost it when one hundred dollars went missing from the paper's subscription account. Maloney sued the priest who fired him, claiming his "character and reputation were damaged." The priest responded by having the police charge Maloney with theft. The judge dismissed the charge after Maloney put on a bizarre display of courtroom histrionics, collapsing in the prisoner's dock and crying out that he wanted "the justice of a British court." After this incident, Maloney turned his back on the Catholic Church and became a Presbyterian.

During the 1920s, with the support of the anti-Catholic Orange Order, Maloney travelled throughout southern Ontario, preaching to crowds about his new religion and denouncing what he saw as the evils of Roman Catholicism. He also wrote articles for the Toronto-based *Sentinel and Orange and Protestant Advocate*, a racist newspaper that called itself "the only distinctively Protestant paper published in Canada." The paper, which enjoyed wide circulation in Alberta, frequently ran discriminatory editorials alleging that European Catholic immigrants threatened the Anglo-Protestant way of life in Canada.

In 1926, while working for the federal Conservatives, Maloney moved to Saskatchewan and tried unsuccessfully to stop the federal Liberals from winning a seat in a Prince Albert by-election. After a brief sojourn in British Columbia, he returned in 1927 to Saskatchewan where, he boasted, he was "destined to make history" by becoming the provincial leader of the Ku Klux Klan.

The Klan had been active since 1921 in Canada, exploiting the divisions between Anglo-Saxon and non-Anglo-Saxon immigrants. The group found support among the Orange lodges in Ontario and British Columbia—as well as in Saskatchewan—for its attacks on Catholics, Québecois, and foreigners. By 1927, however, the Canadian Klan organization was in disarray. Two of the American Klan organizers had absconded with one hundred thousand dollars in Klan membership fees, and a third leader was about to be deported for violating immigration laws. The Saskatchewan Klan was on the point of disbanding when Maloney appeared on the scene. Through skillful oratory, he managed to convince members to carry on under his leadership and work toward the defeat of the provincial Liberals. "Quit and their objectives will be accomplished," he warned.

With Maloney in charge, the Saskatchewan Klan attacked James Gardiner, the Liberal premier, through editorials in such publications as the Orangemen's *Sentinel* and Maloney's own sensationalistic newspaper, *The Western Freedman*. The editorials warned that Liberals were Catholics, that Catholics controlled the provincial education system, that French was being used as the normal language of instruction beyond the legal limit of grade one, and that "foreigners" (i.e., central and eastern Europeans) outnumbered Protestant Anglo-Saxons, having become fifty-three percent of the Saskatchewan population.

The anti-Liberal campaign resulted in what Maloney later called the "biggest surprise in Canadian political history." On June 6, 1929, Maloney's Saskatchewan Klan helped James Anderson's Conservatives topple Gardiner's Liberals. Flushed with success, Maloney began casting around for new political worlds to conquer.

On July 12, 1929, Maloney made a triumphant appearance as the keynote speaker at the Orangemen's parade in Vermilion, Alberta, held annually to commemorate the 1690 victory by King William of Orange over the Catholic James II at the Battle of the Boyne in Drogheda, Ireland. Maloney boasted of his part in smashing the Liberal political machine in Saskatchewan and warned his audience of the "dark cloud that was rolling over the country in the form of immigration." After delivering his standard anti-Catholic rant, he closed by appealing to the crowd to preserve British traditions and connections and to pledge unswerving loyalty to the British flag and to "this great and glorious Canada."

Maloney's Vermilion speech marked the beginning of the Ku Klux Klan crusade in Alberta, although this was not noted in the newspapers at the time. While the Orangemen's parade coincided with the mysterious burning of two crosses in the Vermilion area, neither the Orangemen's *Sentinel* nor the *Vermilion Standard* made any reference to Maloney's Klan connections. Both papers described his speech as being part of an Orangemen's celebration and linked the cross-burning incidents to a local protest over a provincial decision to rename the town of Wellsdale, twenty miles north of Vermilion. A Catholic priest named MacDonnell had brought over one thousand Catholic settlers to the area from Scotland, after which the province changed the name of the town from Wellsdale to Clandonald.

In October 1929, Edmonton newspapers reported that Maloney and his Klan cohorts were active in the province. "Knights of Fiery Cross Plan Invasion of Alberta," said the front-page headline in the *Edmonton Journal.* The newspaper reported that Klan agents were organizing branches throughout the province and planning a big campaign in 1930.

Alberta had a history of prejudice against black immigrants; in 1911 the Calgary and Edmonton boards of trade had passed resolutions urging the federal government to "effectually prevent the advent of Negroes to Western Canada." The province was seen by the Klan as being ripe for conquest. Adding to the Klan's chance of victory was the fact that the province also had a history of discrimination against Chinese, Jews, and central and eastern Europeans, including Doukhobors and Mennonites. A Klan sympathizer told the *Journal* that "contrary to some beliefs, the Klan can perform much good service to the community and that has been proven in other Canadian cities."

Maloney spent the month of July 1930 travelling the Peace River area of northwestern Alberta on a lecture tour sponsored by the Orange Order. The *Sentinel* billed it as an Orange membership drive, but Maloney described it as a Klan organizing tour. He spent the fall of 1930 on a five-month crusade for the Klan in Calgary, where he renamed his *Freedman* newspaper and published it as *The Liberator.*

In September of the following year, Maloney settled in Edmonton with his wife, the former Lenora Elizabeth Miller of Biggar, Saskatchewan. They had married in September 1929, and their daughter Katherine was born five months later. Maloney chose Edmonton as the headquarters for his Alberta Klan operations because, he said, it was the "Rome of the West; the strongest Roman Catholic centre for its size outside of Quebec."

Maloney's first order of Klan business in Edmonton was to work for the defeat of the city's incumbent mayor, James M. Douglas, whom he described as a "puppet of Roman Catholicism." When Labour candidate Dan Knott ousted Douglas by a majority of 3,445 votes in the 1931 Edmonton municipal election, the Canadian Press wire service gave Maloney's Klan all due credit for the Remembrance Day victory. Calgary's *Albertan* newspaper reported that "a gigantic fiery cross, evidently arranged by the Ku Klux Klan, blazed away on the south bank of the Saskatchewan River" after the mayoralty election votes were tabulated. Edmonton police said the burning cross was a Klan victory sign.

Between 1931 and 1932, Maloney lectured weekly on Protestantism at a Legion hall in Edmonton, published *The Liberator,* and held Klan organizing meetings in such places as Camrose, Wetaskiwin, Red Deer, Stettler, and Ponoka. In March 1932, he claimed a major victory when six train coaches of Klan supporters left Edmonton for Wainwright to protest the establishment of a Roman Catholic school district there. In May, he cheered what he saw as the imminent defeat of the Communist-backed Mine Workers Union of Canada in a Crowsnest Pass coal miners' strike, when the Klan burned a cross on the hills of Blairmore and painted a "Reds Beware" sign on the wall of the union hall. In September, Maloney capped what he said was a great year for the Klan in Alberta by applying to the provincial government for an incorporation charter.

Along with his charter application, Maloney wrote a vaguely threatening letter to Premier John Brownlee, who had once donated money to the Klan in what the premier subsequently called "a moment of weakness." "You know, Mr. Brownlee, as well as I do, that the Liberal machine in Edmonton is as bad as the Saskatchewan machine, and will employ any means to hurt you," wrote Maloney. "I went through Saskatchewan and fought master politicians." He hinted that he could make things similarly rough for Brownlee's United Farmers of Alberta if the government did not grant the requested charter.

On September 17, 1932, one day after his letter to Brownlee, Maloney's Klan received its charter, registered under the Alberta Societies Act as "The Invisible Empire Knight and Ladies of the Ku Klux Klan, Realm of Alberta." The objects of the society, as outlined in the chilling words of the document, were to inculcate principles of "Protestantism, racial purity, gentile economic freedom, restrictive and selective immigration, one national public school, and one language, the English language."

Brownlee ignored the advice of his lawyer, Charles Grant, and dismissed the objections of two cabinet ministers when he approved

Maloney's request for a charter. Despite Grant's warning that incorporating a society demanding an oath of secrecy from its members would be contrary to the Criminal Code, Brownlee said "no good purpose would be served by questioning this application." Brownlee never told anyone why he felt the need to support the Klan application.

Obtaining the charter was the high point of Maloney's involvement with the Klan in Alberta. By November 1932, two months after receiving the charter, Maloney was locked in a dispute with another Alberta Klan organizer, Harold Wright, over control of Alberta Klan funds. It had become increasingly clear to Wright that Maloney wanted the money only to finance his personal vendetta against the Roman Catholics in Edmonton. Wright swore an affidavit revealing a "blacklist" of twenty-three prominent individuals that Maloney had targeted for verbal abuse and investigation and delivered the affidavit to Premier Brownlee on December 12, 1932. The list included former mayor James M. Douglas; his successor, Daniel Knott; former Liberal premier Charles Stewart; provincial education minister Perrin Baker; the superintendent of the Royal Alexandra Hospital; the editors of both the *Edmonton Journal* and *Edmonton Bulletin* newspapers; and Charles Grant, the lawyer who had advised Premier Brownlee not to proceed with the Klan charter.

Maloney, in a letter to Brownlee, complained that he was a victim of "one of the dirtiest and lowest plots that was ever concocted against me." A week later, on December 20, 1932, he resigned as Imperial Wizard of the Alberta Klan. "Of his own free will," said Klan lawyer H.A. Mackie. Shortly after that, on New Year's Eve, Maloney broke into the Mayfair Golf Club and set fire to some documents. He damaged his car while trying to escape and later faced a fraud charge for attempting to cover the damage with an insurance claim.

In January 1933 Maloney hit rock bottom, when he was arrested and charged with "administering a seditious oath" contrary to the Criminal Code. In an ironic twist, this turned out to be the Klan oath of secrecy that Brownlee's lawyer had found objectionable. Maloney was also charged in connection with the Mayfair Golf Club break-in and a burglary at an Edmonton law office after he went looking for documentary proof that the Klan was conspiring to get rid of him.

Maloney was sentenced to two months in the Fort Saskatchewan jail for his crimes. In a scene reminiscent of his bizarre courtroom behaviour years earlier, when he was charged with stealing one hundred dollars from the *Catholic Register's* subscription account, Maloney sobbed repentance and begged for mercy. He "threw the police court into pandemonium," reported the *Edmonton Bulletin*, "when he capped his cry-baby plea by falling to the floor in the prisoner's dock."

From that point on, the Ku Klux Klan was a spent force in Alberta. This may be attributed in part to social changes. A slowdown in immigration robbed the Klan of much of its ammunition; it was no longer possible to convince Albertans that the Catholic Church was taking control of Canada. With the deepening economic depression and the coming of war later in the decade, the so-called "Catholic threat" was no longer a concern to Albertans. In fact, as a reader said in a letter to the Wainwright newspaper, "in times of depression, we need our good neighbours." Although the Klan charter purported to strive for "just laws and liberty," it was clear that Imperial Wizard Maloney had a narrower, anti-Catholic agenda, and this agenda ultimately proved to be irrelevant to most Albertans.

Maloney made his final Alberta appearance at a farewell banquet at Edmonton's Macdonald Hotel in October 1933, when he announced that he was leaving for British Columbia. Two years later he published a book entitled *Rome in Canada*, which included an autobiographical account of his life. He later spent time pursuing a stage career in Los Angeles and New York. He died in Toronto in May 1963 of liver disease caused by alcoholism.

Although the Maloney Klan remained incorporated in Alberta until 1952, with an unclaimed deposit of $43.14 at an Edmonton bank, it didn't appear much in the news. The fiery cross remained extinguished until 1972, when a twenty-four-year-old Calgary proponent of "racial purity" named Tearlach Dunsford-Mac a' Phearsoin (Scottish Gaelic for Charles Dunsford MacPherson) became Grand Wizard of a new Alberta Klan, claiming membership of "over one hundred but less than one thousand." The Alberta government, as if reaffirming its 1932 expression of tolerance for John James Maloney's intolerant society, issued a certificate of incorporation to this new organization, which called itself the Confederate Klans of Alberta. Attorney General Mervyn Leitch explained that it was better to keep such groups above-ground, where they could be seen for what they were. The "good sense and decency" of ordinary Albertans would eventually drive them out of the province, said Leitch.

Mac a' Phearsoin's fledgling Klan suffered a series of reverses, first in 1975 when he was convicted of criminal negligence in the shooting death of a Mexican visitor, and again in 1988 when the Klan was publicly implicated in a plot to blow up the Calgary Jewish Centre. In May 1994, Mac a' Phearsoin received a six-year jail sentence for sexually assaulting a young man, and at the time of writing, in April 2002, was facing new sex-related charges arising from a police investigation of activities at a teen drop-in centre. He still owned the copyright to the Alberta Klan name and expressed interest in selling it, but he had no luck attracting potential buyers.

Postscript

In August 1990, a cross-burning incident at an acreage near Provost, Alberta, evoked the racist ghost of John James Maloney for what one hopes will be the last time in this province. The cross-burning was staged by the Alberta branch of the Aryan Nations, a white supremacist group with links to the Klan in the United States. "All Klansmen bring your uniforms," said the invitation to the so-called Aryan Fest. The event attracted extensive media coverage. It resulted in a series of formal complaints to the Alberta Human Rights Commission, followed by a provincial inquiry to determine whether the Aryan Nations and its leader, Terry Long, had violated the anti-discrimination section of Alberta's Individual Rights Protection Act.

The inquiry board ruled in February 1992 that Long and the Aryan Nations had indeed violated the rights protection act and that all the complaints against them were justified. The board ordered the respondents to refrain in the future from—among other things—publicly displaying "burning or lighted crosses, or signs or symbols indicating an affiliation with the Ku Klux Klan." After sixty years of provincial tolerance for the intolerant, the ghost of Maloney was finally exorcised.

Maurice Rupert King

Eccentric millionaire rancher

1897–1996

~

Harrold Augustus King

Eccentric millionaire rancher

1899–1995

They were land-rich, cash-poor millionaires who lived like hoboes—two eccentric hillbilly brothers who disagreed about almost everything yet lived under the same roof for sixty years. Their home was a modest homesteader's shack on a cattle ranch that eventually grew to more than five thousand acres, in the picturesque Porcupine Hills of southwestern Alberta.

The best and most oft-repeated stories about Maurice and Harrold King are the ones that have no basis in fact. It was said, for example, that the brothers always kept a couple of mangy dogs on hand to lick the plates clean after they finished eating because they didn't like to wash dishes. They were also said to have a thing about mice. One popular story says that the roguish pair liked to shock visitors by serving drinking water from a pail with mice swimming in it. Another tall tale has them removing mice from traps, slicing up the carcasses, and serving them to guests as sandwich meat.

Fictional stories aside, it is known that the King brothers had little more than five dollars between them when they first settled in the rolling Porcupine Hills around 1925. Born in England, they were the sons of an alcoholic businessman named Augustus King who made money in the clothing industry. The brothers came to North

The eccentric King brothers, Maurice (left) and Harrold, outside their Porcupine Hills cabin: "With inflation being the way it is, who can suggest anybody's rich?"
(GLENBOW ARCHIVES NA-2864-24350-15)

America with their mother in 1900 and lived first in the Spokane area, where their father was seeking a better life. After six years, the family moved north by train to Alberta and homesteaded near Claresholm.

Though a well-educated man, Augustus King didn't believe in education for his children. "My dad taught me to work because he couldn't see that book learning was much help in earning a living," said Maurice. His father's own "book learning" gave him the means to identify plants and attach to them their proper Latin names, but it didn't give him what he needed to be a successful farmer in western Canada. Instead of starting small and expanding his holdings as he learned, Augustus bought as much land as he could afford and gradually lost it.

Although Harrold never went to school and Maurice dropped out of grade one after breaking his leg, they did acquire some education because their parents taught them to read. They became well versed in biblical scripture and taught themselves carpentry, farm equipment maintenance, and all the skills they needed to survive as trappers and ranchers. Harrold also developed a remarkable talent as a self-taught taxidermist and, as a sideline, learned how to read music. Maurice became adept in matters of business and finance, which became increasingly important to him when the brothers started buying and selling land.

The brothers lived at home until they were in their late twenties, mainly to look after their mother, following a tough, poverty-stricken childhood caused by their father's alcoholism and general ineptness as a farmer. Whenever the boys managed to earn some money, by selling buffalo bones picked from their land or clearing rocks for other homesteaders, their father took the money and spent it on booze. This experience made them reticent in later years about revealing exactly what they owned or how much they were worth. "If they don't know you have it," said Maurice, "then they can't take it away from you."

The brothers wanted to move north and become trappers, but their ailing mother asked them to stay closer to home just in case she needed them. So they walked twenty miles across a mountain ridge to the western side of the Porcupine Hills, staked out a homestead claim, rigged up a tarpaulin tent as temporary shelter, and began fending for themselves. Their modest possessions included a couple of horses, a saddle, an old rifle, and some coyote traps. "We ranched, trapped—did just about everything to keep our bones covered," said Maurice. Tough, resourceful, and fearless, they fed themselves from their root cellar and from the meat of wild animals and amazed their neighbours by roping hibernating bears for sport.

After a year of working and saving, the brothers had accumulated enough money to put a down payment on a quarter section (160 acres) owned by a homesteader who was leaving the district. They built a four-room log cabin in a remote valley on the banks of Sharples Creek, about forty miles north of Pincher Creek, and that remained their home for the next sixty years.

The brothers lived frugally, saved their money, bought horses, cattle, and farm equipment, and gradually expanded their holdings. They even managed to add to their holdings during the Depression, when others were suffering and losing their ranches. By the mid-1940s, the brothers were relatively well off, and the tall tales about them abounded. It was said they hoarded their wealth in tomato juice cans buried around their property and in an old Wells Fargo money sack that they kept under the floorboards of their cabin. It was also said that they spent some of their hard-earned money on a new Model T, started it once, and then parked it permanently in the barn because neither brother liked the sound of the engine.

It wasn't until December 1973, when *Calgary Herald* reporter Ken Hull paid them a visit, that some of the myths about the King brothers began to be dispelled.

No, they assured the reporter, they didn't keep their money in tin cans or in sacks. They either kept it in the bank or invested it in land. But they wouldn't say how much. "With inflation being the way it is, who can suggest anybody's rich?" said Maurice, then a sprightly seventy-six though lame from the broken leg he had suffered as a child. "Maybe forty years ago we would have been wealthy, but the way things are going now we'll be paupers in ten more years."

As for the story about the Model T, Maurice suggested mischievously that the reporter should check the barns before he left. "The only car I remember buying was a six-cylinder Whippet, and that disappeared long ago."

Grizzled and unkempt and wearing worn-out pants held up with binder twine, the aging brothers were creatures of long-established habit. They kept a month's supply of food sitting on their table at all times, admitted to a fondness for chocolates and salted peanuts, and never drank alcohol, only water or green tea. "I tasted spirits when I was seventeen, and haven't got the foul taste out of my mouth yet," said Maurice.

Though they had the means to provide themselves with such modern amenities as indoor plumbing and electricity, the brothers chose to live primitively. Reporter Hull observed that they lived "about twenty-three miles north of Lundbreck, and about seventy-five years behind the rest of the world." A telephone and a battery-operated radio were their only concessions to modern living. For entertainment, they listened to the radio or read from the stacks of old *National Geographic* and *Saturday Evening Post* magazines that they kept piled up on a cupboard. They didn't own a bathtub but did have a wash basin. They cooked their meals on a wood-burning stove that doubled during the day as a furnace. "We don't waste," said Harrold. "We let the stove burn out during the night and light it in the morning. Sometimes, the temperature falls well below freezing in here, but after forty-seven years you get used to it."

Among their many eccentricities was their refusal to open any mail that looked like it might come from the government. Maurice showed Hull two unopened letters with 1932 postmarks. "Actually, there were three that arrived together," he said. "The first one told me the government was seizing a section of land for back taxes, and I figured the others would be saying about the same thing." He didn't like paying taxes and resented seeing his tax money put toward supporting people on welfare.

The brothers were clearly inseparable, wrote Hull, but their relationship was difficult to fathom because they rarely addressed one another directly—each referred to the other in the third person as "the boss"—and they didn't seem to particularly enjoy one another's company. "No, we don't get along," insisted Maurice. "Never have and never will. Can't remember two things in our life that we ever agreed upon." They did seem to agree, however, that they needed one another. At one point, Maurice had left the ranch and bought himself a home in a nearby town because he wanted some comfort, a television set, and electricity. But he sold the place and returned home when his brother refused to leave the homestead. "The boss didn't say much when I returned," said Maurice. "He just looked sort of happy."

Each had once contemplated marriage, but the relationships didn't work out. "Seems the gal I wanted didn't want me," said Harrold. "And those that wanted me—well, I'm just ornery enough that I didn't want them." Maurice said that he too had once been involved with a woman who didn't want to marry him. "After that, I just never felt myself fit to take in a woman."

While their neighbours viewed the brothers as being reclusive, partly because they lived in a remote area, the Kings were in fact quite sociable. Mary-Jo Burles, a Pincher Creek writer who was frequently a guest at their table, found them always ready to entertain visitors and engage in conversation about politics or religion or sex. "I often thought their attitudes a bit naïve but always genuine—they had no guile," she wrote in *First and Second Kings*, a book of anecdotal reminiscences about the brothers.

As the brothers aged into their nineties and were no longer able to look after themselves, they accepted an invitation to move into the home of their hired hands, Russ and Eva Hoffman, who lived on the ranch in a house that was considerably more comfortable than the King cabin. "They reminded me of two old alley cats who had come in out of the cold and couldn't quite believe their luck," wrote Burles. Eva cooked for them and also nursed them through their final illnesses before they moved to the hospital in Claresholm.

Harrold, the younger brother, died in June 1995 at age ninety-six. Maurice died a year later, just shy of his ninety-ninth birthday. His estate owed about $2 million in capital gains taxes. His will dictated that his beneficiaries should include his two nieces, two nephews, and the Hoffmans.

In November 1997, the heirs sold the King ranch at a High River auction that made headlines across Canada. Area ranchers bid on the property hoping they could maintain it as rangeland, while big-city land developers sought to turn the ranch into a collection of recreation properties for urban dwellers. After four hours of bidding, the ranchers won. In all, the land sale fetched $6.325 million for the King heirs. The largest portion of the spread, four thousand acres that included the old King brothers' cabin, sold for $5.725 million to a cattle rancher named Bill Bateman. A smaller, 1,100-acre portion sold for $600,000 to rancher Dave McNalley. It fetched a lower price per acre because it was on the eastern side of the property and didn't have a view of the Rocky Mountains. Both buyers said they respected the wish of the King brothers that the land be kept for grazing purposes. "I take my hat off to the guys who settled this land and the way that they worked it," said Bateman. "That's why I wanted to see it remain as a ranch."

Postscript

In a bizarre footnote to the story of the eccentric King brothers, a fifty-one-year-old squatter named Tysanna Robertson attracted front-page headlines in November 1998, one year after the property sale, when she appeared in a Calgary courtroom to fight an eviction notice. Robertson claimed that the brothers had rescued her from an abusive marriage and had granted her permission to live rent-free in their cabin for as long as she wanted. The lawyers for the estate countered that Robertson had no paperwork to support her claim and that she should find herself another home. The courts sided with the estate lawyers. In September 1999, the Alberta Court of Appeal upheld a lower-court decision and ordered the woman to vacate the premises.

Julia "Big Julie" Kiniski

Edmonton alderman

1899–1969

For close to two decades, Julia Kiniski was something of a joke in Edmonton political circles—the perennial aldermanic candidate who could never get elected. But when she finally won a seat as alderman, in October 1963, this outspoken firebrand was no longer being laughed at. She swept through city hall like an invading army, noisily upsetting the administration and fellow council members with her accusations about uncontrolled spending and graft. Eight months later, the *Edmonton Journal* reported that several of the city's most prominent businessmen wanted "Big Julie"—as the paper dubbed her because of her towering six-foot height—to run for mayor. A veteran alderman responded that if Kiniski were ever elected mayor, he would quit public life for good.

Her dogged determination to win an aldermanic seat was rooted in Kiniski's desire to become the voice of the "little man" at city hall, a place she viewed as a den of corruption and vice. "Those wolves in sheep's clothing are taking the taxpayer to the cleaners while they fill their own pockets with gold," she said in a typical campaign speech. If elected, she vowed, she would become the sole guardian of the little man's dollar in a "pit of vicious self-interest."

Kiniski raised a family and worked to help the needy before becoming involved in Edmonton municipal politics. Born in Poland, she came to Canada with her family when she was twelve and settled in the rural village of Chipman, forty-five miles east of Edmonton. At age sixteen she married Nick Kiniski, a railway section foreman, and they had six children. Julia Kiniski once said that raising her family was one of the things that helped her most as an alderman. "You've got to suffer and sacrifice. You've got to raise a family to know the value of people." The youngest of her children, son

Gene, became internationally famous as one of professional wrestling's so-called "bad guys." The other children included a nurse, a businesswoman, an accordion teacher, a union executive, and a CBC television weatherman, Julian, who later became an alderman himself.

Kiniski also tried raising as a foster child a Native boy who had been arrested for stealing chocolate bars. She eventually had to give him back to the child welfare authorities when he proved to be unmanageable. Though she considered this a failure on her part, she was gratified to receive a Mother's Day card from the boy when he was in his twenties.

During the Depression years, the Kiniskis ran a hotel and then a grocery store in Chipman. In 1937, they moved to Edmonton, where Nick earned five dollars a week as a barber and Julia worked as a cook in a restaurant. Customers said the best feature on the menu was Julia's five-cent soup.

As well as working at the restaurant, Julia also travelled door to door selling cosmetics—"stupid cream and all that stuff," as she called them—and launched her career as a one-woman social welfare agency, advocating at city hall for neighbours who were too weak or sick to leave their homes. A typical story from this period involves the time she undertook to help a woman living on a twenty-dollar-a-month railway pension, whose husband was stricken with chronic asthma and needed hourly injections. Julia bought groceries for the couple and took over the injections. "I suffered with every breath he took," she said. "Every time I gave him the needle I cried."

Another story has to do with the time she visited the office of Social Credit Premier William Aberhart and asked him to donate to a camp for undernourished Edmonton boys. He dug into his pocket and pulled out a two-dollar bill. She rejected the donation as too small and later rejected Social Credit itself because, she said, Aberhart was "insincere as well as stingy."

During the Second World War, Kiniski tried to raise money for the war orphans of her native Poland but was thwarted by members of her own Roman Catholic church. They publicly denounced her as a communist—she was actually a nonpartisan pacifist—and she responded by appealing to some Jewish wholesalers in Edmonton who gave her fifty pairs of shoes. She flew with the shoes to Poland and laced them onto the children's feet herself.

After the war Kiniski switched from selling cosmetics to selling oil shares, using the commissions to buy her own shares and making large profits when she sold them. In 1945, she made the first of her several bids for city council, running as an independent. When she lost that election, she decided she needed more formal education. She enrolled in extension courses at the University of Alberta, walking two miles to class to study psychology, philosophy, and world affairs.

Kiniski continued doing her good works between elections. Her method, she said, was to do things *with* people, not *for* them. "Otherwise, they never learn to do anything for themselves." Sometimes this involved using what psychologists would later call "tough love." Kiniski talked about the time she went into a beer parlour to confront the mother of two small children she had found weeping outside. She berated the mother for her negligence and wouldn't let up until the woman promised to look after her children properly and give up drinking. It was characteristic of Kiniski to be confrontational like this. One of her former "clients," an Edmonton businessman who used to be an alcoholic, told a reporter that the one thing that kept him off the bottle was his fear of disappointing Julia.

When Kiniski finally won her seat as alderman in 1963, she ran as a United Voters Organization candidate and polled thirty-six thousand votes. "Every dog gets his home," she said. "I just got mine." As her reputation grew, so did her following. For the first time in years, people started packing the public gallery of council chambers, hoping to hear the new alderman say something outrageous. Kiniski rarely disappointed them. She warned one alderman that she would "slap you in the kisser if you don't stop interrupting me" and dismissed another as "a midget," which next to her he likely was. A writer for *Maclean's* magazine, Harry Bruce, noted that the "Big Julie" appellation seemed particularly apt. "Her dresses are like chintz army tents, her jewelry like jungle fruit, her fifty-dollar hats like ferryboats."

Bruce characterized her in a 1964 *Maclean's* article as someone who "defends the weak, helps the poor, redeems the outcast, fear-

Julia Kiniski at Edmonton council chambers: "They don't always treat me as a lady. But sometimes I don't act like a lady myself."
(REPRINTED WITH PERMISSION OF *THE CALGARY HERALD*)

lessly confronts the corrupt and, moreover, does all these things without a breath of sanctimony." He added that her "crushing sincerity and her direct, cumbersome English somehow persuade you again, if only for a moment, that the moral rules we learned in childhood are valid, after all. Honesty *is* the best policy. We *should* help our neighbours. We *should* stand up for what we know is right. Perseverance pays. Greed is bad, Courage is good. Love is everything. Julia actually lives by these precepts, and her history seems to vindicate them all."

Kiniski spared nobody her sharp tongue as she embarked on a crusade of looking into things she felt were wrong at city hall. She sneeringly referred to Edmonton's powerful city commissioners as "the troika," addressed a city lawyer as "sonny boy," and dressed him down for using big words. She loved to silence hecklers at public meetings. "I may not talk too good, but you don't think too good," she told one persistent heckler. "Your tongue moves so fast it must have put a knot in your brain."

Overspending at city hall became a particular concern for Kiniski. This proved to be deeply embarrassing for some city officials. In one case, Kiniski forced a city commissioner to disclose the details of his $6,792 bill for a nineteen-day trip to Japan. She studied the receipts, which covered such items as meals, limousines, and gifts for Japanese businessmen, and then she demanded his resignation on the grounds that this kind of spending amounted to "disloyalty." There was no reason, said Kiniski, for the taxpaying public to pay for city officials to "eat canary hearts and have a good time" on business trips.

Kiniski was so conscious of the sanctity of public money that for a while after she was first elected she refused to use official city cars, even when she was representing the city at ribbon-cutting ceremonies. Edmonton aldermen, at that time, were making just eighteen hundred dollars a year. Over the next six years, the aldermanic salary rose to fifty-four hundred dollars, leading Kiniski to propose a controversial motion that the compensation package be cut by ten percent "to set an example for city hall workers." The motion was defeated.

Kiniski annoyed some aldermen to the extent that they refused to attend conventions if they knew she was going too. "They don't always treat me as a lady," she said, "but sometimes I don't act like a lady myself." The less they liked her at city hall, the more the citizens of Edmonton embraced her. A song about her entitled "Hello Julia"—an affectionate parody of "Hello Dolly"—did so well on an Edmonton radio station that it edged out the Beatles for the number one spot on the local hit parade.

In 1964, Kiniski led the charge when Mayor William Hawrelak, who had been forced to resign in 1959 because of dubious land dealings, came under public scrutiny again. Through persistent and aggressive questioning, Kiniski established that the mayor seemed to have an indirect financial interest in a company that was proposing a complicated land swap with the city. The other aldermen didn't like Kiniski's tough line of questioning. "They looked at me like an unwanted dog," she said afterwards. But her persistence in looking into the mayor's affairs ultimately paid off. In 1965, Hawrelak was forced to quit the mayor's office for a second time when it was established that he owned more than a twenty-five-percent interest in a company that sold land to the city for park use.

When Kiniski successfully ran for re-election in 1966, she did so as president of the Civic Rights Protective Association, an organization that she founded to wage battle against the city's attempts to shut down illegal basement suites. This was one time when her concern for the underdog was also a concern for herself. She had personally assisted in ejecting a particularly officious city inspector from her home, and she vowed that she would go to jail before she would let the city shut down her basement suite. "This is my palace, I am the queen," she said. She urged other homeowners to attack the more aggressive enforcement officers with their frying pans, which prompted a formal complaint to council from the building inspectors' union. Yet once again, Kiniski's aggressive methods paid off. By the time she ran for re-election again in 1968, the city had stopped clamping down on basement suites.

Her relentless fight on behalf of the "little man" invariably kept her busy on the phone throughout the day and often past midnight. She took calls from people with legitimate grievances and from cranks such as the woman who wanted Kiniski to silence a neighbour who was repairing his car at 3 A.M. Kiniski suggested that the woman go outside and help the man so that all three of them might get some sleep. Burning the candle at both ends eventually took its toll on Kiniski. During her successful 1968 election campaign, she frequently complained of being "tired out" and also suffered chest pains.

She died in October 1969, at age seventy, after suffering a heart attack. Shortly before her death, she was leading a campaign to have Edmonton's city-owned industrial airport moved out of town and was also seeking to limit Edmonton's population to five hundred thousand. "She was human enough in her faults and great enough that people voted for her," said an editorial in the *Edmonton Journal.* "Her heart was big, her instincts right, and her courage was great."

Her son Julian won her vacant aldermanic seat in the following civic election.

James Henry "Blackie" Audett

Bank robber and escape artist

1902–1979

James Henry "Blackie" Audett was a rebel from Alberta who wrote his name into the pages of American criminal history. He consorted with such notorious mobsters of the 1930s as John Dillinger, Baby Face Nelson, and Pretty Boy Floyd. By his own reckoning he robbed "at least" 120 banks during a career in crime that started when he was a teenager and ended when he was in his seventies. He also made his mark as an escape artist, fleeing custody on several occasions. Yet if we're to believe the autobiographical account of his life, everything might have been different if he hadn't gone to a party on New Year's Eve 1916 and drunk booze for the first time. "That was my first big mistake," he said. He was thirteen at the time.

Audett called Alberta home from the time he was a child until he pulled his first major robbery at age eighteen. Raised on a farm north of Fort Macleod, the son of immigrants from Oregon, Audett had no happy memories of his early childhood. All he could remember were bad things: "Things like my old man flogging me to a standstill with a harness strap when he got drunk. Him hitting my mother with his fist when he was that way. Him and the hired man making fun and mistreating my pony. Things like that can make you bitter. And that kind of bitterness sticks with you."

At age ten, Audett decided he had had enough. After one final beating from his alcoholic father, he packed his belongings, saddled up his pony, Noble, and rode through the night to Calgary. He slept in a livery stable, and the next morning he sold Noble to the stable owner for $150. "I sold the thing I loved the most," he said. "But the money I got for him looked mighty big. Then I went out and got me a job. That was the day I grew up."

He landed a job as "callboy" for the Canadian Pacific Railway, knocking on bedroom doors and waking up train crews when it was time for them to go to work. That's when he received the nickname "Blackie"—referring to the colour of his hair. The railway workers also dubbed him "Ted" because they said he looked like a teddy bear in his coveralls. Newspaper reporters later mistakenly gave his first name as Theodore.

Audett worked on the railway for a year, until his father reported him to the RCMP as a runaway. When a fellow railway worker warned him that the Mounties were at the railway yards looking for him, Audett bought a ticket and climbed aboard a train bound for Spokane, Washington.

He lived in Spokane for two years, working as a switchboard boy at the municipal power plant. He lived at the home of his boss, the chief engineer of the power company, and soon became attracted to his host's thirteen-year-old daughter, Dolly. "We hit it off right from the start," he said. "Dolly was as sweet and smart as she was pretty."

On New Year's Eve 1916, Audett had a choice between going to a party organized by the lineman at the power plant or spending the evening with Dolly. "She had planned we would go to midnight mass, and then head home to fix some popcorn and candy. But when I told her about my invite from the boys, she insisted I go to the party."

That proved to be his downfall. The party was being held at a bootlegging joint on the outskirts of Spokane. Audett didn't want to drink liquor there because of the painful memories associated with his father's alcoholism. But the "boys" insisted that he try some wine. "I had a sip. It tasted pretty good. I had another. And then I guess after that I drank everything in the place."

He awoke the next day "with my head hammering like honky-tonk pianos." Racked with guilt, he couldn't face the prospect of explaining himself to Dolly and her father. "I just wanted to crawl away some place and die." He was standing in an alley, supporting himself against the side of a building, when what seemed like a Good Samaritan in a soldier's uniform came to his rescue, saying, "I know something that will take all your troubles away. What you need is another drink."

Audett spent the day drinking whisky in the soldier's hotel room.

The soldier said he was a sergeant in the Canadian army, and Audett told him he was on the run from Canada's mounted police. After several hours of drinking, Audett passed out. When he awoke, he was wearing a blue band on his left sleeve that said "Volunteer for Service in France." He asked the soldier what was going on. "You have volunteered for duty in the Canadian army, and you are going to fight for the king in France," replied the soldier, showing him, as proof, a document that Audett had signed. Audett protested but to no avail. The soldier told him that if he reneged on his commitment, he would be turned over to the Mounties.

Audett returned to Calgary on the next train. "I was on my way to war. I was thirteen years old, and mighty scared, and mighty homesick."

He did his training at Sarcee Camp on the southwestern outskirts of Calgary. He landed a job driving a staff car for a colonel and hoped this might keep him in Canada for the duration of the war. But he was soon on his way to northern France, where he served as a tank driver and saw action along the Somme and in the Argonne Forest. He was promoted to lieutenant and decorated for bravery after he accidentally found himself behind enemy lines and surprised 260 German soldiers who subsequently surrendered. Audett characterized it as a decoration for cowardice rather than bravery because he was actually trying to avoid the action when he found himself in the midst of it.

Audett renewed contact with Dolly while he was serving in the war. They exchanged correspondence almost daily and talked of marrying when the war was over.

After being hit in the head by bomb shrapnel, Audett was taken to a hospital in Bordeaux and later to a hospital in Winnipeg, where doctors inserted a silver plate in his skull. When he recovered from his wounds, he made arrangements to meet Dolly at a border crossing on the Canada-United States boundary between British Columbia and Idaho, after which they would travel to Spokane for their wedding. But when he arrived at the border crossing, there was no sign of Dolly. He continued on to Spokane, where he learned that she had died just a few hours previously—a victim of the 1918 influenza epidemic. "I guess that was about the last time I ever cried," he said. "When the funeral was over, I just sort of went to hell for a while. I guess I never got over it."

He returned to Calgary after the funeral and went looking for his parents on the farm that he had left at age ten. He wasn't afraid of his father any more. "I figured I was big and rough and able to take care of myself. I was on the other side of seventeen, and an old soldier." When he arrived at the farm, he learned that his parents had divorced and sold the property, and that his mother had moved back to Oregon. He found her in Portland and quickly realized that they didn't have much in common any more. He left after a week and returned to Calgary.

His army back pay ran out after a few weeks. Unable to find a job, Audett embarked on the life of crime that he would pursue for the next sixty years. With four of his ex-army buddies, he made plans to rob a mail train from Spokane that he knew, from having worked on the railway, would be loaded with a bank shipment. "I figured I didn't have anything more to lose out of my life, and it was worth a gamble."

The robbery, at a railway junction about thirty miles west of Calgary, went off without a hitch. The gang tied up the station agent at gunpoint and rearranged the track signals so that the train would grind to an emergency halt upon arrival. When the train stopped, the gang overpowered the crew and piled the moneybags into Audett's Studebaker coupe. They drove back to Calgary and rented a cheap hotel for the night.

The take amounted to $560,000, of which Audett's share was $108,000. He celebrated by trading in his Studebaker for a new six-cylinder McLaughlin touring car. He then moved to Granum, north of Fort Macleod and not far from where he grew up, because he figured he would be safe there.

The law soon caught up with him. Police arrested Audett and one of his fellow robbers at their Granum rooming house and recovered two suitcases full of money that the pair had stashed under their beds. They were held in the provincial jail at Fort Macleod pending a transfer back to Calgary for arraignment and trial.

Before they could be transferred, the two men escaped from custody. They overpowered the guard who was bringing their supper, knocked him out with a brick, stole his clothes and gun, and forced a local garage owner to drive them to Granum, where they stole a car and headed north. At Claresholm, where police had set up road-blocks, they abandoned the car and took off on foot into the Porcupine Hills. Then they borrowed two horses from a friendly rancher and headed toward the Montana border.

The law caught up with the two men again before they could cross the border into the United States. Audett and his fellow robber were returned to Fort Macleod, where they faced several charges, including assault with intent to kill the prison guard. They were con-victed on the assault charge and sentenced to ten years apiece. "It was my first real rap," said Audett. The year was 1920 and he was then eighteen.

Audett served the first part of his sentence in Prince Albert, Saskatchewan, and then was transferred to the penitentiary at Stony Mountain, Manitoba, a fortress-like prison that Audett described as "the Alcatraz of that part of the British Empire." Nobody had ever escaped from Stony Mountain, but Audett was determined to give it a try. "Ten years is a long time," he said.

He made his escape after seven months, riding as a stowaway under the high hood of a prison laundry truck that had been used for service in the First World War. He continued on to the North Dakota border crossing, riding part of the way in a freight train box-car and completing the journey by car. From there he headed west toward Montana, where he planned to get into the bootlegging busi-ness. "There wasn't any way I could get a decent job without tipping everybody off that I was a fugitive from Stony Mountain."

For the next three years, Audett ran booze from the Crowsnest Pass into Montana. He also smuggled Chinese immigrants from British Columbia into Idaho. In 1924, he married a woman named Ethel from Walla Walla, Washington, and tried going straight for a while. He moved to Denver with his wife and worked for a building contractor for about a year. The marriage foundered when Ethel's father found out about Audett's bootlegging activities and ordered his daughter to demand a divorce. Audett moved to Spokane and returned to rum-running.

In 1926, Audett robbed his first bank, in Portland, Oregon. The police weren't able to pin the robbery on him, but they did get him for driving a stolen car across state lines. He was convicted and sentenced to five years at McNeil Island, an American federal penitentiary in Puget Sound, between Seattle and Tacoma, Washington.

Audett escaped from McNeil Island after just five weeks, riding in a speedboat that belonged to the warden's son while the guards in the gun towers were looking the other way. He made his way to Pueblo, Colorado, where he robbed another bank. From there he moved to Bend, Oregon, where he was recognized from a "wanted" poster, arrested as a fugitive from justice, and dispatched by train to the high-security federal prison in Leavenworth, Kansas, to complete his sentence.

Audett never made it to Leavenworth. He jumped from the train near Omaha, Nebraska, was briefly recaptured, and once again escaped from police custody. He headed for Chicago, hooked up with an associate of Al Capone, and spent the next few years robbing banks and cracking safes in Chicago, Detroit, New York, and Kansas City.

In 1929, he sailed to Europe on a fake passport, flush with cash from a bank job he had pulled in Cedar Rapids, Iowa. He made money gambling in Monte Carlo, and then moved on to Bordeaux, where the Sûreté—acting on a tip from the FBI—arrested him and deported him back to the United States. When he arrived at Leavenworth, he was placed in solitary confinement "because I was an escape artist." He completed his sentence, moved to Kansas City, and resumed his career as a bank robber. Other criminals who spent time in Kansas City during that period included John Dillinger, Pretty Boy Floyd, and Baby Face Nelson. "It was like a bank robbers' convention," said Audett.

In 1932, he got married for the second time—this time to a flight attendant named Vi whom he had met in Chicago. He told her he was a cattleman from Texas and said that's why he carried a gun. But she soon figured out what he really did for a living. She told him this didn't really matter to her. "Whatever you are, I love you."

Audett continued robbing banks. His justification for doing this offers a fascinating insight into the criminal mind. The public didn't mind bank robbers, declared Audett, as long as "we acted like gentlemen and didn't hurt anyone." The public saw gangsters as romantic figures, he said, much like latter-day highwaymen or Robin Hoods. "The bankers felt differently about it, of course, and so did the FBI. But people in general, they never got too het up." Every time he robbed a bank, Audett would go to a restaurant afterwards to hear what the customers were saying about it. "It sort of helped to know about that when you were planning your next move," he said. "Like a politician taking a poll." Besides, he added, people didn't care much during the Depression whether banks got robbed or not. "Maybe some of them sort of hoped they would."

In June 1933, Audett witnessed a massacre outside the Kansas City train station that put the lie to any notion the public might have had about gangsters being romantic figures. Mobsters gunned down four law officers in broad daylight while they waited outside the train station to escort an escaped gangster named Frank Nash back to prison in Leavenworth. The United States attorney general responded by declaring a "war against crime" and Audett fled to Chicago to avoid being implicated. A few months later, he was arrested in Oregon for driving a stolen car across state lines. He was sent back to McNeil Island for a five-year stint and, once again, he escaped from the island by boat. After being on the run for two months, he was arrested in Nebraska and sentenced to a total of fifteen years for various offences, including armed robbery.

He was sent to San Francisco's newly opened Alcatraz prison— the Rock, as it was known—from which escape was said to be virtually impossible. Audett didn't even try. He spent the last half of the Depression and the entire Second World War on Alcatraz and was paroled after serving twelve years.

His freedom lasted less than a year. In Oregon, Audett was arrested on a parole violation and sent back to McNeil Island to complete his fifteen-year sentence. This time, the authorities took no chances. They handcuffed, chained, and padlocked him, using a method that later came to be called the "Audett chain." "I never collected any royalties on it," he said wryly.

He was released from McNeil in 1950 at age forty-eight. With no money and no job prospects, Audett turned again to robbery and safe burglary. He was arrested in Oregon, convicted of larceny, and sentenced to seven years at the state penitentiary in Salem. He was paroled after three years, and he told a Portland newspaper that his life of crime was over. "My debt's all paid to society, and I don't intend to run up any more bills."

But old habits die hard. During three months of freedom, before his parole was revoked, Audett was involved in bank robberies in Idaho and Washington. He was returned to prison in Salem, Oregon, where he served another three years.

In April 1953, Audett was paroled again, and he began to write his autobiography in conjunction with a firm of Salem lawyers who had spent two years investigating his story and confirming that his accounts of banks he had robbed and criminals he had known were all true. His parole was revoked before he could complete the manuscript and he finished the book in prison.

The book, entitled *Rap Sheet*, was published simultaneously in Canada and the United States in 1954. Audett wrote that he wasn't proud of the things he did, nor was he ashamed. "No use to be either way." But he did say he would give "everything I've ever owned and everything I ever hope to own" to be back in Spokane on that New Year's Eve in 1916 when he opted to go to a drinking party rather than spend the evening with his beloved Dolly.

Audett continued to live a life of crime during the years that followed. His final brush with notoriety occurred in 1979, shortly before his death from cancer. He was paroled into the custody of crime historian Jay Robert Nash, co-author of *Dillinger: Dead or Alive*. Nash's book claimed that a man shot to death by FBI agents in Chicago in 1934 was not the infamous outlaw John Dillinger—as announced by the FBI at the time—but a Dillinger look-alike whom his mobster friends substituted for the so-called "public enemy number one."

Audett confirmed the substitution theory in an interview with Nash and impressed the historian with his account of his friendship with Dillinger. When Nash published an updated edition of his Dillinger book in 1983, he included an extra chapter about James Henry "Blackie" Audett.

Audett never returned to Alberta after he left during the 1920s to pursue a career robbing banks in the United States. He still has cousins in the Granum area of southern Alberta, where his parents homesteaded, and they recall him with fondness as having been a charming rogue and a "good dancer."

Pete Jamieson

Town crier

1908–1991

~

Arthur Dyson

Jogger

1904–1997

~

Frank Cebuliak

Street pastor

1913–1998

They were downtown street characters who became local celebrities, as well-known in their cities as Edmonton's Macdonald Hotel or the Calgary Tower. Pete Jamieson was Edmonton's self-appointed town crier, the only person ever to hold the job, and he held it for forty years. Arthur Dyson was a marathon runner who jogged through the streets of Calgary wearing a dirty grey track suit and a bright orange fright wig. Frank Cebuliak was a gospel minister who preached outside an Edmonton bank for twenty-five years. All lived for no other reason, it seemed, than to bring a few moments of cheer or reflection into the lives of others during a period when downtowners still had time to stand and stare. These are their individual stories.

Pete Jamieson

It began on a frosty Friday evening in 1935 when *Naughty Marietta*, the first of the movie musicals starring Nelson Eddy and Jeanette MacDonald, opened at Edmonton's Dreamland Theatre. Business was so slow that the cinema manager sent his usher, Pete Jamieson, out onto Jasper Avenue to find some customers. Jamieson shouted out how great the movie was, the curious passersby bought tickets, and a new career was born. For the next forty years, Jamieson was Edmonton's unofficial town crier, a herald who walked the downtown sidewalks advertising movies, sales, and sporting events.

Nobody ever appointed him to the position. Unlike the town crier of Shakespeare's England who was hired by a municipality to proclaim announcements in the streets, Jamieson simply assumed the role and made it his own. "Walk like a soldier," he said to himself, striding along with ramrod-backed military gait, barking out the news and commercials with a sergeant major's roar. As a little boy in Scotland, he had watched soldiers drilling on the barrack square and he admired their style.

Jamieson was twenty-seven when he first took his shouting show to the streets of Edmonton. Born in Dundee, he lived with his parents in Stettler after they moved to Alberta, and he worked variously as a farm labourer, coal miner, bowling alley attendant, and sawmill worker before moving to Edmonton to launch his career as a street performer. Before that, he tried unsuccessfully to join the Canadian army for no other reason, he said, than a desire to march on parade.

For the longest time, Jamieson was able to make a good living on the streets. Store owners paid him five dollars a month to clean their sidewalks and advertise their wares. Entertainment promoters paid him $1.50 a day to pitch their events. "Cheaper than radio advertising," he said. If they didn't pay him in cash, they paid him in headgear. He had a hat or cap for every occasion, as many as four hundred when he counted them all. He had a hockey cap to wear on hockey night, a football cap for football night, and a party hat to wear on May 4. "Good news today," he would shout on that day. "It's my birthday."

Jamieson's workday began shortly after 1 A.M., when he left his downtown rooming house and set out to sweep the summer's dust or winter's snow from the sidewalks outside Edmonton stores. A city bylaw decreed that all downtown sidewalk cleaning had to be done before 8 A.M. so Jamieson had plenty of business. He worked until 6 A.M., returned to his rooming house for breakfast, and then reappeared on the streets with megaphone in hand to promote store specials, ball games, wrestling matches, and other events. "Well, friends, we're back to bingo tonight. Eight-car bingo, 8.30 sharp at the Edmonton Gardens. Don't blame us if you don't win a car." For good measure, and at no extra cost, he would throw in a newscast and a weather forecast, courtesy of his pals at the radio station. "Winds out of the northwest at fifteen miles an hour, gusting to twenty-five. Cool today with scattered showers." He liked rain, he said. "It keeps the old megaphone clean." He didn't work Sundays, and he hated public holidays. "Everything's closed and the streets are deserted," he said. "Never good for business."

Jamieson did his town crier routine throughout the day, with an hour's break in the morning to listen to the testimony being given in magistrate's court—"It's very educational," he explained—and a much longer break in the afternoon to drink beer and tell jokes at the Ambassador Hotel. Because he was a popular downtown character, everyone wanted to buy him a drink. He kept his voice in shape by downing a glass of hot water last thing at night and first thing in the morning. "The louder I shout, the clearer I sound," he said.

During the 1950s, Jamieson claimed he was the only town crier in Canada and brought his show to CJCA Radio, where an accommodating announcer named Jim Hand invited him to tell listeners what was going on each day. When Hand, as a joke, decided to run for mayor, he appointed Jamieson as his campaign publicist and the result was one of the most entertaining series of election announcements ever aired. When CJCA eventually decided to replace Jamieson with a paid commercial, the public outcry was such that the station had to put him back on the air. It was only when Hand died in 1962 that Jamieson's broadcasting career came to an end. By then he had become something of a national celebrity, written up in newspapers and magazines. "He is a Jasper Avenue institution," said *Weekend* magazine. "Colourful, genial, irrepressible and—to some sober folk—slightly disreputable." With his bushy white beard, distinctive military gait, and colourful headgear, he was one of Edmonton's most recognizable characters. When he appeared in the Klondike Days parade, he drew as many cheers as Klondike Mike, the city's popular mascot.

Jamieson "retired" from the streets when he was in his sixties, which is to say that he stopped getting paid for his public appearances because the stores and entertainment promoters no longer needed him. He continued to walk the streets anyhow because he liked being outside and meeting people. "Advertising is free nowadays, I do it as a hobby," he said. But it was clear that time was passing him by and that Edmontonians were starting to view him as something of a public embarrassment. A 1978 National Film Board documentary, *Never A Dull Moment*, showed Jamieson on his daily rounds, shouting out the news and weather to people who turned their backs on him and handing out the city's promotional pamphlets to bored-looking passengers on a bus. "He seems to be an Edmonton eccentric in a booming city that no longer has time for eccentrics," wrote John Dodd in the *Edmonton Journal*. "People who get their news on cablevision have little use for a town crier."

Jamieson continued to make occasional appearances downtown as he aged into his seventies, though injuries to his knees impaired his walking, and he was no longer able to deliver the news and weather with the parade-square thunder of days past. "I'll continue as long as the Man above keeps me alive," he told a reporter who visited him at the nursing home where he now lived. His final appearance, memorably captured in a photograph on the back cover of the *Edmonton Access Catalogue* city guide, occurred when the catalogue's publisher, Allan Shute, asked him to pose next to a recently demolished downtown high-rise. "I waved my hand and the building came down," said the caption.

When he died in 1991, at age eighty-two, Jamieson was remembered as a symbol of an earlier Edmonton, a kinder and gentler place, where street people were accepted rather than marginalized. "Pete was an eccentric, likable, and a man of his times," said Edmonton historian Tony Cashman. "Howling on Jasper Avenue nowadays would be like crying in the wilderness."

Arthur Dyson

Calgary first discovered Arthur Dyson in 1972 when, at age sixty-eight, he won the over-sixty seniors' section of the *Calgary Herald* Road Race. "They tell me I own the world record for the marathon for sixty-eight-year-olds," he said. He had taken up marathon running at age sixty-five to lose weight, and he planned to keep doing it until someone put him in the *Guinness Book of World Records*.

The youngest son of a Lancashire, England, dentist, Dyson was separated from his siblings and raised in orphanages from age ten onward when his father succumbed to alcoholism and his mother was stricken with dementia. He remained a ward of the British child welfare system until he was in his teens. At that point, he became one of the "orphans, waifs, and strays" plucked from his homeland and shipped across the sea to a land where clean air, hard work, and healthy discipline would contribute to his wholesome development.

There were thousands like him, orphans and abandoned children who were shipped to Canada, Australia, and other parts of the British Empire as part of a human export scheme that historian Kenneth Bagnall has called "one of the most Draconian movements in the history of emigration." For Britain, it was a cheap way of dealing with the problem of surplus children while at the same time populating the colonies with good British stock. For Canada, it was a cheap way of building up the workforce.

Dyson worked as an indentured farm labourer in Ontario ("two years slavery to pay back the passage at three dollars a month") and then spent five years travelling westward across the country, picking up casual work wherever he could.

He arrived in Vancouver in 1929. "Everybody was broke, including myself," he said. "But when it got real tough, the Vancouver police would give the down-and-outers vouchers for clothes and a shave. If you needed a meal, you could have it upstairs in their depot." He became what he called a "tourist," riding the boxcars to wherever he might find a bed and a hot meal. "No rest for the wicked. Had to keep moving."

At age thirty-five, Dyson tried to enlist for army service in the Second World War, but he had fractured his leg in a farm accident and that ruined his chances. "I told them I could run and walk, but

Arthur Dyson on the road: "I told them I could run and walk,
but I would not guarantee it on uneven ground."
(GLENBOW ARCHIVES NA-2864-31,241-31A)

I would not guarantee it on uneven ground." He spent the war years working in the bush northwest of Edmonton, near Whitecourt.

Dyson drifted for several years after the war and eventually landed in Calgary, where he lived on the streets. During the summer and fall he slept on a park bench by day and jogged the Calgary streets at night. In winter, he jogged during the daytime and spent his nights at the homeless shelter. When the temperatures dropped to twenty below zero, he jogged indoors, through the downtown's Plus-15 skywalk system. He made for a strange sight—wizened, toothless, with chicken legs and an orange wig that looked like it was borrowed from the Ronald McDonald clown.

His running exploits kept him in the news through the 1970s and into the 1980s. Newspapers described him as the oldest active marathon runner in Canada and the fourth oldest in the world. In the winter of 1985, he had to give up running for a while when he froze a toe while sleeping outside during a cold snap. The toe had to be amputated, and Dyson moved into a nursing home to recuperate. But before long he was back downtown, riding the train in the light rail transit system's free-fare zone and using his pension cheque to buy meals at the city hall cafeteria.

Dyson's running finally came to an end in July 1987, when he suffered a broken leg while jogging near his nursing home in the city's northeast. He was then eighty-three. He had never won his way into the *Guinness Book of World Records*, but he did win his way into the hearts of the nursing home workers who looked after him during his final years. "He is very vibrant and a bit eccentric," said one staffer after Dyson had staged one of his many "escapes" from the nursing home, leading to police missing-person reports and stories in the newspapers. "We let him stay here even though he doesn't follow rules, such as obeying curfews."

In his late eighties, Dyson revealed a long-hidden talent for playing the piano. He had studied music for six years at the Lancashire orphanage, and he still had the touch. "When they hear my piano playing, they are going to sit up and take notice," he told a reporter who visited him at the nursing home. "Put that down." The reporter confirmed that Dyson really could play.

When Dyson died at age ninety-three, he left no known survivors. He had long lost touch with whatever family he might have left behind in England. "Basically, the staff on the fourth floor were his family," said a nurse at the George Boyack nursing home. "He was pretty special to us."

Frank Cebuliak

He was never particularly religious in his younger years, when he lived on a farm near Red Willow, east of Stettler. Nor was he particularly religious after he married and moved to Williams Lake, British Columbia, to become a cowboy. In fact, he told people he was a communist and an agnostic. Then suddenly, in his fifties, Frank Cebuliak underwent a spiritual conversion and became an evangelical Christian. He quit his job as a road builder, left his wife and four children behind in Vernon, B.C., and hitchhiked to the Yukon, preaching the gospel as he went. "I witnessed on foot to every miner, prospector, trapper, hunter, and river driver in the Dawson City area," he said. "God told me to."

He arrived in Edmonton in 1972, chose a downtown street corner for his pulpit, and began preaching. Dressed neatly in suit and tie with a raincoat and stylish fedora, he sometimes preached alone and sometimes preached with friends he considered "filled with the Holy Spirit." "May I offer you a testimony of what Jesus did?" Cebuliak would ask passersby, handing a leaflet to those who stopped to listen. "God has been preparing Edmonton for a long time now. Edmonton is close, on the verge of becoming a spiritual Jerusalem."

Sometimes he spoke of a bright future for Edmonton. At other times, he saw only doom and gloom. "There will come a day when no airplanes will move, when there will be no more fuel or electricity and no food to eat," he told an *Edmonton Journal* reporter. "Within an hour the Earth will be gone and there will be silence." Cebuliak said he didn't fear the apocalypse himself because it would lead to eternal life.

While many Edmontonians paid little heed to Cebuliak's street-corner proclamations, a few did stop to chat—an average of seventy-five a day in summer and twenty-five a day in winter—and found him to be good-humoured, calm, and approachable. He had opinions on many subjects aside from religion, including city politics. When asked what he thought of the disgraced mayor William Hawrelak, found guilty of "gross misconduct" because of his involvement in shady land deals, Cebuliak replied that Hawrelak was a good man. He had known him when they were both active as lobbyists with the Alberta Farmers' Union, and he felt that the mayor was meant to serve. "God can use Hawrelak," he said.

He didn't mind if people ignored him. It had become his calling to preach the word of God, and he preached it regardless of whether or not anyone was listening. Nor did he mind if people became angry at him. On one occasion he was posing for a photograph when a drunk came up and punched him in the mouth. "That was the second time I have been struck in the service of my ministry," said Cebuliak, his clear eyes shining. "God drew us all together on this street corner and had you take a picture."

He preached for eight hours a day, six days a week, in all kinds of weather. "The cold weather only goes so far with me," he said. "When it gets to thirty or forty below, faith takes over and I don't feel it any more." Faith had healed him of cancer after doctors told him there was no hope, he said, so he believed that the Lord was always looking after him.

For some years, Cebuliak lived with his daughter and son-in-law in Edmonton's Steele Heights district, preaching to the passengers on the No. 12 bus as he headed home after a day's preaching. Later on, he lived in a downtown rooming house. It was easier that way, he said, because his family didn't really approve of his lifestyle. "Ministering is sometimes a hard thing to do when your family isn't behind you," he said. "But it's not so hard for me because I know I'll be saved." He had to separate from his family, he added, because "they haven't received the faith."

Cebuliak refused to accept welfare or a pension cheque, saying the Lord would provide. "I used to preach part-time in a church and I always found I was short of money. So I gave it up and now I get along just fine." He survived on contributions from supporters, who gave him enough to pay for his rent and food. When heart problems and other ailments began to slow him down in his eighties, he did agree to accept the pension, and at his son's encouragement he moved into a seniors' apartment. But he still went downtown every day to preach. The home care caseworkers urged him to rest, but preaching was Cebuliak's calling.

Cebuliak died at age eighty-five. An obituary notice in the newspaper showed that while his family might not have endorsed his lifestyle, they did understand what he tried to do in life: "Frank didn't just dream of becoming a cowboy, he became a cowboy. Nor did he just dream of becoming a minister in the service of his Lord, he became that minister. There are many men who dream their lives, but few men, like Frank, who live their dreams."

Don Mackay

Disgraced Calgary mayor

1914–1979

History rarely forgives politicians who blot their copybooks. Don Mackay would like to have been remembered as the mayor who gave Calgary its white hat symbol and turned the Grey Cup weekend into a national festival. Instead, he is remembered for having "borrowed" a load of city-owned cement to pour the basement of his holiday home in Banff. A judge reprimanded him for making improper use of his position as mayor and the voters kicked him out of office when he ran for re-election.

Before his fall from grace, Mackay was one of Calgary's most effective elected salesmen, an energetic hustler who wore a white cowboy hat, gave hats to visiting dignitaries, and worked hard to convince petroleum companies after the big 1947 Leduc oil strike that they should put their head offices in Calgary, not in Edmonton.

The origins of the white hat as Calgary's civic symbol go back to the summer of 1946, when a local rancher and oilman named Bill Herron Jr. bought four white-felt cowboy hats from Smithbilt Hats for his family to wear in the Stampede parade. The next summer, more than two hundred Calgarians, including then-alderman Mackay, bought white Smithbilt hats to wear during Stampede. The year after that, the white hat went national when a rowdy crowd of three hundred Calgarians, led by Mackay, wore the hats to the 1948 Grey Cup game in Toronto to cheer on a couple of dozen football players from Calgary.

Mackay had been in municipal politics for three years when he brought the raucous spirit of the Stampede to what had previously been a routine Canadian football final with a parade thrown in. Born in Lethbridge, the son of an alcoholic newspaperman, Mackay lived in Drumheller from age ten onward. He got his first taste of public life at age sixteen, when he appeared before Calgary city council as the Drumheller delegate from the Alberta Tuxis Boys, a youth parliament organized by the United Church. At age eighteen, Mackay left Drumheller and moved to Calgary. He spent a year selling advertisements and subscriptions for the old *Albertan* newspaper and then became a sports announcer with what has since become CFXL Radio.

Mackay's on-air exuberance and idiosyncratic use of the language made him a popular announcer, even with people who didn't normally listen to sports broadcasts. His unorthodox play-by-play accounts of hockey, baseball, and football games made him one of the best-known radio personalities in the city. If a play seemed particularly silly to him, he would characterize it as "supercilious." If it seemed dangerous, or perhaps aimless, he would call it "half-hazard." If a visiting player had an unusual last name, Mackay would mock it. After describing a home run hit by a Saskatchewan catcher named Petrunia, Mackay said, "And speaking of petrunias, the ones in my garden are great this year."

Mackay joined the Calgary Junior Chamber of Commerce to improve his public speaking skills and made his first bid for elected office in 1945, when he was thirty-one. He topped the aldermanic polls. But city hall didn't see much of the newcomer during his first two-year term. He was also elected provincial and then national president of the Jaycees during that period and the demands of those positions, coupled with his full-time job as manager of the radio station, left him with little time for civic matters. Calgary voters didn't seem to mind. In the next election, they again put him at the top of the polls.

In November 1948, Mackay accompanied three hundred Calgary football fans and half a dozen horses and chuckwagon drivers to Toronto for the Grey Cup game. His glad-handing, "howdy-pardner" style attracted national headlines when it was rumoured that Mackay rode a horse through the lobby of the Royal York Hotel after Calgary's 12–7 victory over Ottawa. (Two others also claimed credit for the fabled hotel ride: Calgary football player Woody Strode and rancher Bill Herron Jr.) "It could have been the greatest lost weekend of all time," said Mackay. "But a few of us got together and

Mayor Don Mackay with his trademark white hat:
"It was a mistake in my life that I wish I had never made."
(Glenbow Archives NA-2775-1)

decided to make something of it. I sort of inherited the job of master of ceremonies on the train journey down there."

Showmanship also defined the style he brought to the mayor's office when he won the election in 1949. He made his white hat the only headgear he would ever wear and, in the words of a friend, "set out to convert the whole world to Calgarianism." The mayor's job, declared Mackay, was to function as Calgary's most ardent civic booster. "I was out to promote the image and the potential of the city," he said. "I laid the foundation and watched others build the structure."

There were some who thought a mayor should be more than a public relations flack. Aldermen questioned his habit of presenting white hats to every visiting dignitary, including the Duke of Edinburgh, who received one for every royal visit and eventually started giving them back. Aldermen also accused Mackay of "too much running around the country" and told him he should spend more time in his office. Plus, they wondered about his commitment to the city when he ran twice—unsuccessfully—as a federal Liberal.

The voters didn't care about any of this. For ten years they remained solidly behind the mayor with the white hat and the ready smile. Then suddenly Mackay's political career came to an end, with the heavy thump of thirty-five cement bags. A story in the weekly *North Hill News* mentioned no names, merely asking, "What city father had his basement poured with city cement?" Mackay admitted sheepishly to council that he had "borrowed" the cement for his holiday home in Banff and then forgotten about it. With tears in his eyes, he asked for council's understanding, but council called for a judicial inquiry.

The judge's report could not have been more damning. Mackay had to explain his acceptance of gifts—plane trips and other largesse—from developers and firms doing business with the city. "I was filled with anger and frustration at the twists and turns that people would put on things," he said. "You do something and it seems all right, but somebody else sees it and they make something completely different of it. It was a mistake in my life that I wish I had never made. It deprived me of a double opportunity. I would have liked to have gone on in the public life of Canada. And that was a door that closed on me."

The judge's inquiry concluded that Mackay had "derived a direct improper advantage through his position as mayor." But Mackay believed he had done no wrong. He had accepted favours after the fact as thank-you gestures for facilitating developments that he felt were in the best interests of the city. An alderman named Jim Macdonald called on council to remove Mackay from office, but his fellow aldermen didn't think the mayor's admitted indiscretion was "improper" enough to warrant impeachment. "You're either pregnant or you're not pregnant," retorted Macdonald. "There is no such thing as being a little bit pregnant." He resigned his own council seat in protest and, in the 1959 municipal election, the Calgary electorate had its say. For the first time ever, Mackay lost a mayoralty race. Harry Hays, who subsequently had a civic building named after him, won by 1,478 votes. "It was a shattering experience. I was a crestfallen man," said Mackay. "It put me into two years of about the worst mental depression that a man can take. Luckily, I didn't break."

He tried to start over in Calgary. He rented jukeboxes. He founded a public relations firm with the white hat as its emblem. Finally, he moved to Phoenix, where he tried to promote curling as a winter sport. It was difficult. The people in Arizona laughed when Mackay showed them a video of men with brooms chasing rocks. But things gradually improved. By 1962, three years after his fall from grace, Mackay was director of the Phoenix Development Association. He became an American citizen. In 1969, the Phoenix mayor called him "a very outstanding Phoenician" and gave him a key to the city.

Mackay returned from exile five years later, working first as a sales representative for the Calgary Convention Centre and then selling real estate. His flamboyant style was unchanged. Mackay drove a Cadillac with a white hat in the back window. "More people than ever are moving to Calgary," he said. "You've got to sell them the Calgary way of life."

Mackay died in 1979, at age sixty-four, after suffering a stroke. The obituary stories all made reference to the so-called "cement scandal." "He erred in judgment," wrote *Calgary Herald* columnist Merv

Anderson. "The price of error in politics is higher than in almost any other sphere of human activity." At his political peak, Mackay had enjoyed unrivalled popularity doing what he believed was right for the city. In the end, he was remembered as the politician who put his own interest ahead of the interests of the citizens. He paid dearly for forgetting the adage that elected officials must avoid even the appearance of impropriety.

Fred Perceval, Earl of Egmont

Reluctant nobleman

1914–2001

He was born a rancher and he died a rancher after sampling the glass-bowl life of a British nobleman and deciding it was not for him. Frederick George Perceval, eccentric and reclusive, opted to live in obscurity as the proprietor of the Two-Dot Ranch in Nanton, south of Calgary, rather than take his rightful place in the House of Lords as the eleventh Earl of Egmont. One wonders what Conrad Black and other commoners who have coveted seats in England's ermine-bedecked upper chamber might have given to trade places with Perceval.

A descendant of Sir John Perceval, the seventeenth-century Irish peer who cofounded the American colony of Georgia, and of Spencer Perceval, the only British prime minister to die by assassination, Fred Perceval grew up in genteel poverty in the foothills near Priddis, where his father and grandfather finally settled and homesteaded after emigrating from England to Iowa and then to Alberta in the 1880s. Fred's mother, one of the first nurses at the Holy Cross Hospital in Calgary, died of pneumonia in 1916 when the boy was two years old. His grandmother cared for him until she died in 1922. After that, Fred was raised by his father, who said he wanted the boy to be "reared in the clean, hard ways of the Canadian West."

In 1929, the lives of father and son were suddenly disrupted when England's ninth Earl of Egmont, a widower without children or near relatives, died at his castle home in Ringwood, Hampshire. The title passed to his Canadian cousin, Fred's fifty-five-year-old father, who hadn't lived in England since he was seven years old and knew little about his genealogy. "It's hard to pick up and leave after living in Alberta for thirty years," said the father. "I love this little ranch, my cattle and my horses, and I'm not going to leave it unless it is absolutely necessary." Young Fred wasn't impressed by the change in family fortunes either. "You taught me to read and write, and you taught me to ride and shoot," he told his father. "We've got a nice home here, and I don't want to leave it." However, the estate matters in England had to be settled and so they left.

After a sale of their possessions in which the boy's two dogs sold for twenty-five cents each and his saddle pony fetched $3.25, they set sail for England. When they landed, they were besieged by reporters, who couldn't get enough of the "backwoods heir" and his "Jackie Coogan" son. The newspapers had no shortage of advice for the new earl on how to conduct himself as a peer of the realm. They criticized his cloth cap and ill-fitting suit—"they look as if they were bought in a hurry at a general store in a country market town"—and told him that anyone who could learn to be a rancher could also learn to be an earl.

The story took on the dimensions of a soap opera when two equally colourful characters stepped forward to claim the Egmont title. One was a baker from north London who said he was born in Australia as the son of the sixth earl's brother. The other was a retired Lancashire optician who claimed to be descended from the fifth earl. Both cases were dismissed in court. When debts and death duties forced the new earl from Canada to sell some of the family silver and pictures, the optician pretender created a scene at Christie's auction house by loudly declaring that the sale items belonged to him. Security staff quickly removed him.

The new earl tried to avoid further newspaper publicity by retreating behind the walls of Avon Castle, with its private railway and thirteen hundred acres. There, he and fourteen-year-old Fred set out to recreate the atmosphere of the two-room ranch house they had shared together in Alberta. They dismissed the servants and moved into the kitchen, where they spent their days and did their own cooking for the next three years. They closed the castle gates, shuttered the windows, and refused to have anything to do with their country neighbours.

A Canadian reporter visited the pair in April 1932, after hearing that the earl had put the castle up for sale and that he and Fred might be returning to Canada. "I have been treated with nothing but injus-

The Percevals, father and son, on their Priddis ranch in 1929, shortly after learning about their inheritance: "We've got a nice home here and I don't want to leave it."
(GLENBOW ARCHIVES NA-16-285)

tice since I came here," the earl said bitterly. "Claimants to the title have worried the life out of me, and now there are death duties and other burdens." He had already sold many of the family heirlooms, and now he planned to dispose of the castle, leave England, and go travelling with his son.

A month later, the earl died in a car crash near Southampton after visiting the farm in Warwickshire where he was born. Newspapers called him "the loneliest peer in England" and said he had seemed bewildered and ill at ease among the splendid surroundings of his inheritance. "The late earl's accent and manners may, like his boots, have been a shade too thick for the fine carpets of Hampshire," said the *Sunday Express*. Son Fred, at age seventeen, succeeded to his father's title and became the eleventh Earl of Egmont. The "boy earl," as the press immediately dubbed him, inherited £211,000 from his father plus an additional £150,000 from a dowager aunt—more than enough to cover the outstanding death duties on his father's estate.

The young earl returned to Calgary in July 1933 as a guest of the Stampede board and gave a long interview to the *Calgary Herald* about his life as an English peer. He hated the constant press attention—"I spend half my time running away from reporters and photographers"—and he resented newspaper reports saying he was living in an "impoverished condition" on his Hampshire estate. "We have enough money in the family to keep up the estate four times over," he insisted. The castle and estate were still up for sale, and he didn't know if he would remain in England—where he enjoyed riding his motorcycle along deserted country roads at eighty-five miles an hour—or return to the Priddis ranch where he rode horses and felt more at home. "What English people do not realize is that there is a greater spirit of freedom and generosity over here in Canada," he said. "Canada gets into one's system and, although it is nice to go away for a time, it is good to get back."

By 1934, Fred seemed to have decided to remain in England, at least for the time being. He had married his second cousin, a nineteen-year-old dental nurse from Calgary named Geraldine Anne Augusta Moodie, and she enjoyed being the new Countess of Egmont. She wasn't of noble birth herself, but she was descended from Canadian frontier aristocracy. Her grandfather, Major John Douglas Moodie, was an inspector with the Royal North-West Mounted Police and a governor of the Hudson's Bay Company. She was also descended from Lieutenant James FitzGibbon, a British hero of the War of 1812, and from Susanna Moodie, the legendary nineteenth-century Canadian author whose life was recreated in a major poetic work by the writer Margaret Atwood.

Fred turned twenty-one in 1935, and press reports said that he was now content to live the life of an English gentleman for the sake of his one-year-old son, who would eventually inherit his title. He talked about buying a London townhouse and eventually sending his son to Eton. There was even some suggestion that Fred might take his seat in the House of Lords, but that seemed to be more press speculation than fact. He would, the newspapers said, be "the only member of the House of Lords who could rope, throw, and brand a steer." When asked about his plans, Fred angrily replied, "I don't know why I should tell my private affairs to the newspapers."

In July 1938, the *Calgary Herald* reported that Fred had "definite plans" for taking his seat in the House of Lords. Three months later, the paper reported that Fred had sold Avon Castle to a wealthy London property surveyor for eighty thousand pounds and that he and his family were returning to Alberta. Finally exasperated with the media attention that had followed him for nine years—he had reached the stage, said the *Herald*, of "not merely turning his back to the camera but wanting to smash it"—Fred gave what would be his last press interview. He had built a twenty-six-room ranch home on the southern outskirts of Calgary, in what is now the Willow Park subdivision, and that was where he and his family planned to live. They would farm 680 acres, raise cattle, barley, and wheat, and be known simply as Mr. and Mrs. Fred Perceval and family. There would be no more interviews, no more photographs, no more living in the glare of the media spotlight.

Perceval remained true to his word. There were no more stories in the press until 1950, when his youngest son died at age four after a long illness. There were further headlines in 1959 when the ranch property was sold to make way for the Willow Park mall and housing development, and Perceval told an English newspaper that he might consider moving back to Britain, where he still had land at Epsom. Instead, the Percevals moved to west of Nanton, to a five-thousand-acre ranch property once owned by the Earl of Minto, governor general of Canada from 1898 to 1904.

Perceval continued to avoid the press for the rest of his life. When Canada's constitution was "patriated" by the repeal of the British North America Act in 1982, a reporter phoned the Perceval home to ask if Fred would go to England to speak in what was expected to be a controversial House of Lords debate. Mrs. Perceval answered the phone. "You can't speak to him now," she said. "He's out doing his chores." The reporter said he would call back later. The countess said the reporter shouldn't bother because her husband would refuse to come to the phone.

In 1999, when Perceval was eighty-five, his daughter Geraldine told a reporter that her father was almost deaf and saddened by the death of his wife four years previously. But otherwise, said the daughter, he was in good health, still hardy enough to drive a tractor. "He still works the ranch, just like he has for years," she said. "He was always a rancher before he was an earl."

The reluctant earl died at his Nanton ranch in December 2001. Neighbours told the newspapers that it was hard for them to think of Perceval as a belted earl when he appeared on his ranch in bib overalls with six days' growth of beard and a dusty hat. He had asked them to address him as "Fred," but they always called him "the Earl" behind his back. And they said he once surprised them by saying he really wished he could have taken his seat in the House of Lords instead of returning to Alberta. His title passed to his son, Thomas Frederick, who said he would continue to live on the family ranch near Nanton.

Richard Johnston

Music educator and arts advocate

1917–1997

He was loud, brash, argumentative, and confrontational. He dressed like a cowboy and he cursed like a longshoreman, both of which caused heads to turn whenever he appeared at a recital or concert. He was also the most passionate advocate for music education and the most energetic champion of Canadian chamber and orchestral music that Alberta has ever seen. The music might sound like burps and squawks to some listeners—including him—but he never failed to support it. "This must take place," he said.

His name was Richard Johnston. A self-styled "incurable romantic," he was born in Chicago, into a family of American-Swedish Lutherans who were not, he said, especially musical, though his mother did play the piano for family singsongs. Johnston studied piano as a child and began to take music seriously when one of his junior high school teachers introduced him to members of the Chicago Symphony and encouraged him to compose. He subsequently studied composition with Nadia Boulanger, an influential French conductor and composer. Together, in 1944, they presented the world premiere of Stravinsky's *Sonata for Two Pianos*.

By the time he took his first teaching job, at Luther College in the Nebraskan town of Wahoo (which he pronounced with the gusto of a hockey cheer), Johnston was a committed supporter of music education for young people. "The clarinet should sing, the piano should sing, the percussion should sing. And above all, the child should sing," he said. "We must concern ourselves with the proper education of young children in terms of music, arts, and drama. Proper growth can happen only if a high enough beginning standard is set."

Johnston moved to Canada in 1947 to work as professor of music, theory, and composition at the University of Toronto. By then he had a sizable number of compositions to his credit, most of which he later pulled from his catalogue because he considered them inferior. Boulanger had taught him that there is only one standard— "good or not good"—and "so I will never allow my string quartet to be played in public again. It was once dear to me but no longer represents me."

Johnston spent two decades in Toronto, married a concert pianist named Yvonne Guiget, and had four children who were, he said, musically talented. "I think most children are talented until it's knocked out of them." Johnston did not, however, immediately appreciate the specialized talent of one of his students, R. Murray Schafer, who later achieved an international reputation as a composer of "soundscapes." Both strongly opinionated, the two clashed as teacher and student. Johnston, in his characteristic confrontational style, banished Schafer from his classes. But in equally characteristic style he subsequently acknowledged Schafer's brilliance as a composer by seeking money for the acquisition of his papers by the Canadian Music Centre, a Toronto-based repository of scores and recordings.

By the time he arrived in Calgary in 1968, to assume a position as dean of fine arts at the University of Calgary, Johnston had become an enthusiastic collector of Canadian folk songs, a composer in the folk idiom, and an acerbic commentator on cultural matters for CBC Radio. Calgarians soon got a taste of his critical style when he did an interview with the *Calgary Herald* and said most of the commercial and public buildings in the city were "ugly insults to the eye and the imagination." "Call them shelters, call them warehouses, or efficient parking places for typewriters and filing cabinets," he said. "But don't call them examples of good architectural thinking. I find almost nothing here that is worthy of the name architecture." He suggested that a panel of architects and artists be commissioned by city hall to approve plans for new buildings. An anonymous *Herald* editorial writer was moved to protest. "Most Calgary citizens will be in stark disagreement with the university dean," said the editorial. "It is our judgment that a great deal of imagination and variety is represented in the outward appearances of the buildings that have been sprouting up in the downtown area."

Educator and composer Richard Johnston:
"I think most children are talented until it's knocked out of them."
(COURTESY CANADIAN MUSIC CENTRE)

When he did his second interview with the *Herald*, in 1970, Johnston was no longer critical of downtown architecture. He declared that the buildings were now of only passing concern to him because eventually they would disintegrate. "But the fine arts won't disintegrate," he said. "The thoughts of Plato and Homer are still vital after all these centuries. We're dealing in the lasting ideas, those elements of life that make for continuity from age to age." He had visited Hungary twice to study the music education system developed by the composer Zoltan Kodály, and he had come to believe that children should be exposed to good music at the earliest age possible for the sake of their cognitive development. "The Hungarians have taught their people how to read music, perform, and listen intelligently to music," said Johnston. "Until we do it over here, we're not going to make the kind of progress we must make as a civilized society."

Johnston finished his five-year term as arts dean in 1973, when he was fifty-six, and he spent the next ten years teaching music at the University of Calgary, promoting the educational theories of Kodály and advocating for the cause of modern music. There was nothing discreet about his method; he used the word "stupid" more than any other. The schools were "stupid" for not recognizing that music literacy was as important to the development of a child's mind as the ability to read books. Concert organizers were "stupid" for only rarely featuring modern music in their programs. Musicians were "stupid" for not wanting to play it ("they say it mucks up their ears"), and audiences were "stupid" for not wanting to listen to it.

Johnston did more than complain about the situation. Together with composer Violet Archer, he formed the Alberta Composers' Association—the first such provincial organization in Canada—and he organized festivals to showcase the music of young Alberta composers. He set up a western branch of the Canadian Music Centre at the University of Calgary and delighted in telling people in Toronto how much good music was being produced "out here in the boonies, in the shadow of the Rockies." He edited several collections of songs for use in schools, actively encouraged orchestra boards and music societies to program new works, and helped organize a provincial song contest to celebrate Alberta's seventy-fifth anniversary in 1980.

With all his various educational and organizational activities, Johnston left little time for his own composing. But he still managed to create a small body of highly regarded works for orchestra, piano, chamber, vocal, and choral groups. "My life as a composer has always taken a back seat to other talents and practical needs, but has always been there as a unifying thread in everything I have undertaken," he said. "I have a passionate loyalty to the creative side of life and believe it generates more important details in our personal and public lives than any other single talent. If we are not all Bachs or Schuberts, we can at least learn through our own serious efforts the pleasures of creativity and the appreciation of the efforts of the masters."

Johnston's musician friends acknowledged his contribution as a composer by presenting a concert of his works at the University of Calgary in 1987, to celebrate his seventieth birthday. The Hungarian government gave him a medal in recognition of his twenty-year struggle to create interest in the Kodály method of musical education, and he received the Order of Canada in 1997 for making music "a living part of the experience of Canadian children." By then the semi-retired educator and full-time gadfly was nearing eighty and was still "running pretty fast." "I'm an old man, for God's sake, I can't afford to go slow," he told the *Calgary Herald*. "I've got a lot of things to do and not much time left." He was composing a song cycle for its premiere performance in Belgium, contributing articles to the *Encyclopedia of Music in Canada,* and travelling back and forth to Europe to serve on various music committees. "Retirement doesn't mean desiccation, you don't have to fall apart," he said. "You have to keep working, you have to keep doing things. If life is meaningful to you, then you have to do meaningful things. I do the kinds of things that are meaningful to me." He said he appreciated receiving the Order of Canada, "but I just do what I want to do."

Johnston died six months later. A friend said his energy and passion for music sustained him to the end. "Sometimes he would go down the wrong street—that would be difficult for the people in the way, he had this energy for going forward—but he did make things happen. He was a catalyst for action."

Elizabeth "Sweaty Betty" Abbott

Slum landlord

1919–1989

On Edmonton's skid row, "Sweaty Betty" Abbott was hailed as a saviour for providing rental housing for welfare recipients and cursed as a villain for confiscating their government cheques to ensure she got her rent money.

Abbott became Edmonton's most notorious slum landlord of the 1970s and 1980s after first establishing herself as a successful restaurant operator in the city. Born in the rural community of Edgerton, Alberta, southeast of Edmonton near the Saskatchewan border, she was one of six children raised in a two-room shack without plumbing or electricity, and she learned about recycling before the word became part of everyday language. The dresses she wore as a child were old flour sacks with the Robin Hood brand name removed.

Married and divorced by her early twenties, Abbott moved to Edmonton in her thirties, worked as a cook and waitress, and then opened a downtown café that she named "Betty's Lunch." She kept it open twenty-four hours a day, charged low prices, and became a kind of mother figure to her employees, who were mostly young, single women living away from home for the first time. Abbott listened to their problems, encouraged them to be independent, and told them she would never tolerate loose morals.

A shrewd businesswoman, Abbott invested the proceeds from her restaurant in some rundown houses in Edmonton's inner-city West Delton neighbourhood, southeast of the municipal airport, and rented them out to poor people. The sign on the door of "Betty's Rentals" said she welcomed "Métis, Natives, and Coloureds." She never turned a prospective customer away, not even when the person had a reputation for trashing property. If a tenant kicked the doors down, Abbott would leave them down. If the person smashed windows, she would board them up. "No point in fixing them, they'll only get broken again," she said.

As her restaurant business grew, Abbott acquired more rental properties. Eventually she owned three restaurants and a total of thirty-eight houses. Ten of the houses were in a district that the locals called "Sesame Street" because it was always a hive of police and social worker activity. Many of the residents were drug and alcohol abusers, and violence was common in the neighbourhood.

Abbott never spent any money on fixing up her dilapidated properties. The only work she ever did on them was to paint the outsides bright yellow or orange, using surplus paint from the local public works department. Inside, she left the houses in the ramshackle condition in which she had found them. She wouldn't spend money on furniture because she figured the tenants would only sell it for liquor, and she wouldn't spend money on repairs to floors or walls because many of her renters were chronic house wreckers. This posed an interesting dilemma for Edmonton's social workers. Should they have the bylaw officers move in and close her down, or should they leave well enough alone? They decided to leave well enough alone. If Sweaty Betty's homes were condemned, many derelict families would be left without a place to live.

Because she never turned anyone away, Abbott was a godsend to the social workers. More than once they were thankful for Sweaty Betty's help—not only did she provide accommodation for clients with no place else to turn, but she would also lend them money if necessary. She would delay charging them rent until their government cheque arrived, buy food for their children, and bail them out of jail when they got drunk and disorderly. But she also made it clear that every cent she spent on them had to be returned to her on payday. That meant Abbott became both loan officer and banker, cashing the government cheque, taking what she was owed, and doling out the rest in small amounts. A tenant could always get money from her to go to the grocery store but never to visit the liquor store.

Abbott was perhaps the best kind of landlord. She was caring and considerate toward those with legal, emotional, and financial problems, and tough as nails when it came to handling abusive husbands, drunks, and drug addicts. "You have to be tough when you go into your rental house and you find fourteen teenagers stoned on glue and little kids sniffing gasoline," her lawyer, Bill Craig, told an *Edmonton Journal* reporter. "You go and look at Betty's houses, and you think that this landlord should be put in jail. But then you look a little harder and you discover that nobody wants to have anything to do with the people who put the houses in that condition."

Some said her rents were exorbitant, at the top end of what the welfare authorities would allow, but most agreed that she could hardly be faulted for this because her houses were the only accommodation option available for people otherwise impossible to house. Plus, her maintenance and cleanup costs were considerable whenever the houses were vacated. "They wrecked those houses," said one social worker. "Betty had to take a shovel to clean out the living rooms, and often it was human waste."

Abbott didn't live in any of the houses herself. For many years she lived in a comfortable apartment with good furniture, a stereo system, and a fine collection of dance music albums. She liked dancing and sometimes taught classes at the YWCA. Then, in the 1970s, she sold her restaurants, moved out of her apartment, and set up house in the backroom of her rental office. She said it was to be just a temporary arrangement until she found another apartment, but she ended up staying there until she died of a heart attack in February 1989 at age sixty-nine.

Her only concession to luxury at the end of her life was a pink Cadillac. Otherwise she lived in the same kind of squalor as her tenants. Though her properties were estimated to be worth more than $1 million, and she talked about eventually cashing in and buying a nice house for herself, Abbott ended her days in a tiny bedroom crammed with stored paint and carpets and linoleum. "When she died, she was living in abject poverty," said lawyer Craig.

Her properties were divided among various family members who had no interest in maintaining them as rental housing. The for-sale signs started appearing in the front yards a few weeks after her death. "It's now impossible to find homes for the hard-to-house," said an inner-city worker. "Betty Abbott's houses needed to be fixed up, and they needed to have everything working. But now we don't have them at all, and we have thirty-eight families without a place to live."

John Kushner

Politician and dispenser of malapropisms

1924–1984

John Kushner is remembered in Alberta political circles as a wily rogue who—during almost thirty years in public life—scored some dramatic political victories followed by humiliating failures and more than a few moments of controversy. He is also remembered for his physically imposing presence—a big unpolished rawboned man with hands like meat cleavers and the muttonchop sideburns of a riverboat gambler. But it's for his malapropisms and his fractured syntax that Kushner is probably best remembered, especially by the reporters who covered him first as a Calgary alderman, then as a provincial MLA and federal MP, and who eventually elevated him to the ranks of the "forever quoted." Here are some gems from the Book of Kushner as gathered by various reporters over the years:

—"I don't want the information, I just want the facts."

—"It's high time we upgraded grade one to kindergarten level."

—"I want to hear from the expertise."

—"I'm not talking about businessmen, I'm talking about people."

—"Well, don't get your dandruff up."

There were many more where those came from. "One of the country's leading malapropists," author John Robert Colombo wrote admiringly when he decided to include Kushner in one of his celebrated collections of Canadian quotations. Kushner claimed to be fluent in five languages and, if he spoke them all in the same idiosyncratic way that he spoke English, he must have left them laughing from Vladivostok to Vegreville.

His first languages were Polish, German, and Russian. Born in Poland, to an Austrian-Ukrainian father who saw service in the First World War and a Russian mother who worked as a seamstress,

Kushner came to Canada with his family in 1930 when he was six. He couldn't speak any English when he started school. "I went to school bare-footed," he recalled after he entered provincial politics in 1971. "I never dreamed that one day I would be taking a plane to work."

The family homesteaded near Innisfree, in the Vegreville area east of Edmonton. Times, said Kushner, were hard. During the Depression, the family was on relief. "We didn't call it welfare then, it was relief—and it was." He quit school in grade ten and worked as a farm labourer for a year before joining the Canadian army to serve in the Second World War. After the war, he visited Calgary to see the Stampede, took a liking to the city, and decided to stay. He married a young woman named Olga, worked as a carpenter with the Canadian Pacific Railways (CPR), then joined the Calgary public school system as a locksmith. After he went into politics, he boasted that he still retained his locksmithing skills: "If I can't pick any lock in less than a minute, whoa, I'm in trouble."

His political life began in the labour movement where, as a CPR employee, he rose through the ranks of the Brotherhood of Railway Trainmen to the Calgary local presidency. He also served as president of the Calgary Labour Council. In the community, Kushner served as president of the Bridgeland Community Association and was active in ratepayers' groups and little league baseball. "What are we living for if not to help one another?" he said.

In 1955, at age thirty-one, Kushner made his first, unsuccessful, bid for city council. Ten years later, on his seventh try—sometimes as an independent, sometimes as a labour candidate—he finally won an aldermanic seat. "Nobody's going to pull the rug out from inside my shoes," he told reporters as he prepared to take his seat. When he added, "I'm speaking off the cuff of my head," the reporters knew that Kushner would always be good for a quotable quote on a slow news day.

Was it an act, or was Kushner really given to ludicrous misuse of the language? The journalists seemed to think it was his canny way of courting the working-class vote. "He's dumb," said one reporter, "like a fox."

In June 1966, eight months after being elected, Kushner became

the first alderman in forty-three years to be ejected from city council—for refusing to withdraw an allegation that his fellow councillors
were influenced by outside pressures. "You quietly made your points,
loud and clear," he told one alderman before council voted to eject
him. "Would you please sit down and let me be patient?" He
resumed his seat at the next meeting, without apologizing.

Kushner decided in 1967 to take a run for the mayor's chair.
When his "Push for Kush" campaign failed, the embittered Kushner
refused to congratulate the victorious Jack Leslie. "We were fighting
a political machine, a money machine," he told reporters. "I should
congratulate the machine?" He sat out that year without a place on
council, but returned triumphantly in 1968 when two anticipated
candidates failed to file for election and Kushner won the aldermanic
seat by acclamation. He worked on several people-oriented campaigns, such as fighting bus fare and zoo admission increases, but not
all the people approved of his style. "Watch out for Kushner," said a
woman who worked with him. "He'll give you half a finger but take
ten in return."

Controversy dogged Kushner in 1970 when police were called to
investigate what became known as the "Apple Tree Incident." He was
accused of removing an apple tree from an urban renewal site and
having it transplanted to the front lawn of his son's Calgary home. A
judicial inquiry found that Kushner acted innocently but "by his
indiscretion he cost the city a great many lost man-hours and made
fools of the police." Council narrowly defeated a censuring motion.
"We're making a mountain out of a mole," said the relieved Kushner.

Kushner cut his ties with organized labour in 1970, cancelled his
membership in the provincial NDP, and announced his intention to
run provincially for the Conservatives. "We need more of a labour
voice in the government," he said enigmatically. Later he added,
"Let's face it, people vote for the Tories." However, they didn't vote
for Kushner, at least not right away. In August 1971, when Peter
Lougheed's Tories swept to power in the provincial election, Kushner
lost the race in Calgary McCall to the Social Credit candidate,
George Ho Lem. It would take another four years before Kushner
would try again to gain a provincial seat.

Kushner returned to the municipal arena after losing provincially, and won his third term on council in October 1971. He also won a seat on the public school board, becoming the first Calgarian to hold two civic offices simultaneously. He remained on the board until 1974, and ignited a furor when he and his fellow trustees voted themselves a 50 percent pay increase. He subsequently quit as a trustee and was immediately hired by the board for a newly-created position as security officer. A few months later, in October 1974, he lost his aldermanic seat in the civic election. "My biggest plans for now are to relax," he said. However, two weeks later, he ran for the provincial Tory nomination in Calgary Mountain View and won on the third ballot.

Kushner's financial life was as much of a roller-coaster as his political career. A car-rental agency he ran went belly-up, leaving him badly in debt. Election campaigns also drained his resources. "I lost everything when I ran for mayor," said Kushner. "I don't do this to get rich, that's for sure." There were a number of court judgments against him for failure to pay debts, and his school board wages were garnisheed.

Kushner won the provincial riding of Calgary Mountain View in March 1975 in a narrow victory over Socred candidate Albert Ludwig, who accused Kushner of "corrupt practices" during the campaign for donating twenty gallons of root beer to a community association. After two years in Edmonton, Kushner sought and won the federal Tory nomination in Calgary East in June 1977, but the national party rejected his candidacy because of irregularities in memberships sold by his supporters. One membership was registered to a dead woman, and at least three people held multiple memberships. Kushner shrugged off the rejection, and returned in October of that year to regain the Calgary East nomination. He stepped down as MLA (his son Stan won the Tory nomination to succeed him) and went on to win the federal seat in the May 1979 general election when Joe Clark became prime minister.

At every level of politics Kushner found himself characterized as a loose cannon and was shunned by political colleagues. During his early years as an alderman he alienated fellow councillors when he claimed they were controlled by the Tories. When he became a Tory MLA, he found it hard to be taken seriously by other Tories because he had been identified with the NDP and organized labour for so many years. In Ottawa, he sat on the backbenches, kept a low profile, and participated in very few of the Commons committee meetings that fill the lives of most MPs. "I'd like to see that the committees are meaningful and that you're not just wasting your time there," he said. "I'm here to represent the people who wanted me here, so they could be heard."

At times Kushner seemed more like an ordinary citizen than a politician, and he carefully cultivated that proletarian image by making it appear that he was just a regular guy who stumbled into the corridors of power. "I'm no different from my supporters, we're the same kind of people," he said. A political colleague described him as "the kind of guy you'd like to have living next door." His strength lay with the working class, the ethnic groups, and the labourers, who might not remember his name but always recognized him as one of their own. However, Kushner's political foes saw him as being little more than an opportunist with an ability to "totally forget his philosophy and be on the popular side of every issue." Nick Taylor, the former provincial Liberal leader and later senator, characterized him as "a little like a cross-eyed discus thrower. You never know where he'll hit."

Kushner died in office, the sitting MP for Calgary East, at age sixty after a short battle with bowel cancer. During his five years in Ottawa, he had denounced Parliament as a "complete farce" and the Commons committee system as a "zoo." But he was committed to serving his constituents because of his unwavering conviction that they wanted him there, representing their interests and giving voice to their concerns. His philosophy, as articulated in a typical gem from the Book of Kushner, was that "there's only one taxpayer—you and me."

Elizabeth Jane "Bettie" Hewes

Politician and social activist

1924–2001

Bettie Hewes was the original "raging granny" of Alberta politics, a single-minded member of the provincial Liberal party, once described by Premier Ralph Klein as "one of the most formidable foes I ever had." With her snow-white hair, half-glasses, and pearl necklace, Hewes looked the part, and when she spoke she sounded it. "She was only rabid when she knew she was right," said her son Rob. "And she always knew she was right."

The "granny" references first appeared in the press in 1994, when Hewes at age seventy assumed command as interim leader after provincial Liberal leader Laurence Decore resigned. She was happy to wear the description like a badge of honour. "I am a great white granny," she acknowledged in an interview with the *Calgary Herald*. "And I can be ruthless when I need to be."

Her ruthlessness came from a fierce desire to make governments accountable to the citizens who elect them. Born in Brampton, Ontario, Hewes worked as an occupational therapist before becoming a social activist. She moved to Edmonton in 1949 with her husband, William, a chemical engineer, and spent the next twenty-five years volunteering with community organizations, including a two-year stint as executive director of the Canadian Mental Health Association.

Hewes's political career began in 1973 out of concern that Edmonton city council was devising grand schemes for freeways instead of transit systems, to the resulting detriment of Edmonton's river valley and inner-city neighbourhoods. She organized the Urban Reform Group Edmonton (URGE) as a watchdog organization to keep tabs on city planning. In 1974, she was elected to council as URGE's aldermanic candidate.

Hewes spent ten years on council, supported construction of Edmonton's municipal railway system, and helped dismantle an old-boys' network at city hall when she lobbied successfully to have power shifted from the secretive board of appointed departmental commissioners to an executive committee of elected aldermen. Hewes later served on the executive committee, which involved helping manage what was then the second-largest municipal corporation in Canada, just behind Montreal. That's why she was offended in 1984 when the federal Liberals unexpectedly appointed her chairman of Canadian National Railways and the opposition Conservatives said that she wasn't qualified for the job. "I have helped manage the city of Edmonton, a $1.5-billion operation which runs its own utilities," she insisted. "And that's very considerable experience." But it was clear, nonetheless, that the CN post was a patronage appointment. Few were surprised when she lost the job after Brian Mulroney's Conservatives rose to power in September 1984. "One likes to think one would be removed for cause—which would be incompetence or immorality or fraud," said Hewes angrily. "But I think I did a good job of being the chairman." She made a point of wearing a red dress—the traditional Liberal colour—when talking to the press about her firing.

In 1986, Hewes moved into provincial politics and was elected Liberal member of the legislative assembly for Edmonton Gold Bar. Being a Liberal in Alberta at that time could get one barred from every cocktail party in town, but Hewes was respected for her work on city council and won handily in the election. She increased her majority in subsequent elections. When elected to her third term in 1993, Hewes received more votes than any other Alberta MLA—including the newly elected premier, Ralph Klein.

When provincial Liberal leader Decore stepped down in July 1994 after losing two elections to the Conservatives—first under Don Getty and then under Klein—Hewes became interim leader. She soon showed her strength as Opposition critic by leading the fight to kill a controversial bill that would have allowed private corporations to deliver public services while setting their own user fees and pollution standards. Hewes denounced the bill as an "insidious program not only to dismantle accountability but to dismantle parliamentary democracy." She pressed her point in a radio debate with Stockwell Day, who was then government House leader. Day let the bill die and later said Hewes was the "only person I can think of who strikes fear in my heart." Nobody, he said, "wants to take on Alberta's grandmother."

Klein didn't want to take her on either. When she scolded him for appointing then-deputy premier Ken Kowalski to a $110,000-a-year government patronage position, Klein quickly rescinded the job offer. He was also embarrassed when Hewes exposed a secret $100-million loan guarantee negotiated by his government. "She has a fierce sense of social justice," he said. "The government's activities simply feed us some great opportunities," responded Hewes.

After she had spent five months as temporary Liberal leader, Hewes's supporters encouraged her to run for the permanent position, but she was now seventy-one and didn't feel like being ruthless any longer. "I know I have the capability to do that, but I'm not going to put myself in that position," she said. "I choose not to." Besides, she wanted to play the "granny" role her thirteen grandchildren liked best: puttering in her garden, sewing handicrafts, and cooking Sunday dinners.

Grant Mitchell became Liberal leader, and Hewes did not run in the 1997 provincial election when Klein's government won its second mandate. But she remained active behind the political scenes, chairing a committee at a provincial economic conference and surprising some people by calling for the government's $1.2-billion surplus to fund a tax cut. Had she followed the traditional Liberal pattern, Hewes would have asked for increased spending on social services. But she figured a tax cut was probably inevitable and said that individuals—not corporations—should get the break. The government actually went along with the idea and announced a small cut in personal taxes for Albertans in its 1998 budget. Needless to say, Hewes never received credit for suggesting the idea.

Hewes retired to Brockville, Ontario, and died in November 2001 at age seventy-seven. Stockwell Day was one of several politicians who remembered her as much for her "raging granny" attributes as for her commitment to social justice. "Some of us were getting a little nervous that she might be the next Liberal leader," said

Day, recalling his time as an Alberta cabinet minister before he became leader of the federal Canadian Alliance party. "She would certainly have been the toughest opponent we could have faced."

Horace "Bud" Olson

Rebel politician

1925–2002

Bud Olson first served notice that he was going to be a maverick politician in 1967, when he cut his ties with the federal Social Credit party and crossed the floor to join the Liberals. From then on, until he left public life in 2000, Olson continually courted controversy. He even managed to get into trouble after being appointed Alberta's lieutenant-governor in 1996 when his predecessor, Gordon Towers, publicly criticized him for moving the traditional New Year's Day viceregal reception from Edmonton to Medicine Hat, closer to Olson's home. "He's not a lieutenant-governor any more, I don't give a damn what Towers thinks," retorted the outspoken Olson. "I'm going to hold it in Medicine Hat."

Olson was a rancher before he became a shoot-from-the-lip public figure. He was born on his father's ranch near Iddesleigh, about thirty miles northeast of Brooks, and descended from Norwegian pioneers who homesteaded in South Dakota before moving to southern Alberta. Nicknamed "Buddy" by his family, Horace Olson grew up during the Depression and "until my late teens, I hardly knew what money looked like. It was almost a cashless society." He boarded in Medicine Hat for high school, working part-time in a greenhouse for twenty-five cents an hour, and started cattle ranching in his teens on land acquired by his father. He saved his money and, when he could afford it, purchased his father's general store in Iddesleigh "at no bargain price." Like his father, he became a supporter of the provincial Social Credit party and later the federal party.

Olson first ran as a federal Socred in 1957 at age thirty-one, driven by a belief that the way to win elections was to campaign harder than one's opponents. Against all expectations, he won, but

Senator Bud Olson on his Medicine Hat ranch: "All my life
I get into trouble all the time for saying what I think."
(REPRINTED WITH PERMISSION OF *THE CALGARY HERALD*)

he served only one year and lost his Medicine Hat seat in the 1958 Conservative sweep led by John Diefenbaker. Olson regained the seat in 1962 and was re-elected in 1963, when the Diefenbaker government collapsed over the issue of nuclear weapons on Canadian soil. Olson was again re-elected in 1965. He established a reputation for himself as a relentless critic of Liberal government policies on issues ranging from drug prices to coal subsidies. A colleague characterized him as a "bulldog" in debate. Olson said that his job as an Opposition member was to "plot and scheme the overthrow of the government."

When the federal Social Credit party died as a national force in 1967, Olson jumped to Lester Pearson's Liberals. The move surprised many because the political winds in Alberta were blowing strongly in favour of the federal Tories. But Olson, who described himself as an "unrepentant pragmatist" decided he had a better chance of making a difference with the Liberals, who held no seats in Alberta at the time. "Joining the Conservatives didn't seem very attractive to me," he told the *Edmonton Journal.* "I had a choice of either getting in the lineup there or joining the Liberals and being number one right away. I decided that being number one was better." His motto, he said, was "Think wrongly if you please, but in all cases think of yourself." The Liberal he had defeated in the 1965 election, Jim Miller, predicted Olson would lose his seat in the next election. Instead, Olson squeaked through by a 116-vote margin in 1968 and was named minister of agriculture in Pierre Trudeau's first cabinet.

Some expected that Olson, with his lack of executive experience, would do poorly in the technically difficult and politically dangerous agricultural portfolio. Trudeau had established the confrontational tone of Ottawa's attitude toward the West by asking struggling western farmers, "Why should I sell your wheat?" But Olson did just fine, thanks. He refused to be lured into compensating western farmers for surplus production. Instead, he introduced controversial legislation setting production quotas for grain and established marketing boards for the turkey and chicken industries. "I told farmers their job was to participate in marketing and not expect someone else to do it for them," he said afterwards. "Farmers needed to be active to get a good price." Farm organizations opposed his method, fearing a loss of control over agricultural policies, but Olson prevailed and the marketing agencies were here to stay.

By the time the 1972 election came around, Olson was seen as one of the few Trudeau ministers who had performed to general satisfaction. But he lost his seat anyway, swept away by the growing anti-Trudeau sentiment on the Prairies. Two years later, he lost again. Olson went back to the land, worked behind the political scenes, and served on the Economic Council of Canada. But he longed for the action of public life, and when Trudeau offered him a Senate seat in 1977, he accepted. By 1979, during Joe Clark's brief reign as prime minister, he was opposition house leader in the Senate.

In 1980, a resurrected Trudeau was ascendant again in the Commons and Olson gained new power in the Senate as minister of state for economic and regional development. In that role, he had the unenviable task of selling Trudeau's unpopular National Energy Program to the West. The NEP was a controversial interventionist policy aimed at increasing Canadian ownership of the oil industry, and Olson attempted to make it palatable by setting up a committee of oil and gas industry representatives to advise the Liberals on regulatory reforms. "You can bash me all you want," he told the committee's disgruntled members, "but we've got to make this work." He later told reporters that the big oil companies were "no more than branch offices that take instructions from their head offices outside the country. We do not want to be controlled by the whims of corporations based outside the country."

While supporting government intervention in the case of the NEP, the unpredictable Olson defied his cabinet colleagues by opposing government bailouts for companies faltering because of poor management. He also refused to support the government's industrial strategy of pouring huge sums of money into the high-technology sector, and he was influential in reducing the federal aid given to Chrysler Canada from $750 million to $200 million. "Sometimes you have to decide if you should wet-nurse an industry that's doing very well without it," said Olson. "We have to give free enterprise the maximum opportunity to perform."

From 1982 to 1984, Olson served as government leader in the Senate. He won over dubious cabinet colleagues by keeping

Canadian Forces Base Suffield open when the defence ministry wanted to shut it down and by pushing through the Canadian section of the Alaska Highway natural gas pipeline when the United States government wanted to cancel the entire project. After that, with Brian Mulroney's Conservatives in power, Olson stepped away from the political limelight—though he did battle the government on the Goods and Services Tax—and took on a new role as unofficial ombudsman for Albertans. "I'm not trying to replace the lawyers or even the MPs," he said. "But some people who have problems with the government feel that it's less partisan to go through my office."

When he emerged from political obscurity in 1996 to accept the appointment as Alberta's fourteenth lieutenant-governor, Olson again found himself in the midst of controversy. Some patronage critics suggested that Olson only got the $92,000-a-year job because of his friendship with Prime Minister Jean Chrétien. Olson shrugged and said, "You know, that might even be true." But he hastened to add that his predecessor, Gordon Towers, had been given the post because he was a friend of Brian Mulroney and a supporter of Mulroney's first Conservative leadership bid.

Olson first caused a stir as lieutenant-governor when he said that he might use his viceregal powers to block spending plans by the Alberta cabinet. He noted that the Klein government regularly approved millions of dollars in controversial spending by special warrant—without scrutiny by the legislature or Opposition debate—behind the closed doors of cabinet. "That, to me, is wrong," said Olson. He said that unless he was dealing with an emergency spending situation, he would delay indefinitely any special warrants that crossed his desk. "It would be very tempting not to sign them," he said.

Olson's three-year tenure as lieutenant-governor is perhaps best remembered for the war of words that erupted with former lieutenant-governor Towers when Olson abandoned a ninety-year tradition and moved the New Year's Day levee—an informal public reception at which the guests consume tea, biscuits, and "moose milk" (rum and eggnog)—from Edmonton to Medicine Hat. To compound matters, Olson asked his niece in Medicine Hat to cater the event. Towers accused Olson of disgracing his office and called on him to resign. Olson dismissed the resignation call as "crap" and dismissed Towers as a "lightweight with no influence on anybody that counts." Asked by reporters if he also used the word "damn" in his response, Olson replied, "Of course. It's a good expressive word." Afterwards, in another departure from traditional viceregal diplomacy, Olson told an *Edmonton Journal* reporter, "All my life I get into trouble all the time for saying what I think. And some people seem to think that there's a certain way that the lieutenant-governor is supposed to act and talk, and that he can't stray from that at all. Well, that's their opinion and they're welcome to it. But I don't necessarily agree with it, so I'm going to say what I think, and I expect to be in trouble all the rest of my life."

Trouble continued a few months later when reporters discovered that Olson had used government aircraft sixteen times during his first three months as lieutenant-governor—four times more than Towers had done over the corresponding period a year earlier. "Even Her Majesty has attempted to keep in step with the public mood by trimming her costs and travelling on commercial aircraft," said the *Calgary Herald* in an editorial. "It would be appropriate, therefore, for Her Majesty's representative in this province to follow the Royal lead and ensure that he is thrifty and frugal with the little people's money. Surely, sir, that is not too much to ask." Olson did not respond.

Olson made news in April 1997 when he predicted that Alberta's expected surge in population growth would bring "a whole lot of socio-economic problems." His name was in the headlines again in September of that year when he learned that the viceregal flag could not be flown at half-mast to mark the death of Diana, Princess of Wales. Olson ordered that the flag be taken down completely. "It looked disrespectful at the top of the pole," he said. "You don't find protocol for unique situations, so you have to make it up."

Olson was supposed to serve as Alberta's lieutenant-governor until 2001 but he resigned suddenly in December 1999, citing poor health. He was replaced by noted horticulturist and author Lois Hole, who said that she would be moving the New Year's Day levee back to Edmonton. Olson chose not to give a farewell speech in the legislature, as Towers had done, nor did he attend Hole's inauguration ceremony. "It's her party," he said. "I had my party four years ago." He said he would spend his retirement helping his son, who farmed near Medicine Hat.

Olson died in February 2002, at age seventy-six, after suffering a stroke. "Alberta politician was always a maverick," said the headline in the *Globe and Mail.*

Tommy Common

Singer

1933–1985

❧

D'arcy Scott

Broadcaster

1933–1993

During the 1950s, when they were in their early twenties, Tommy Common and D'arcy Scott were just the male stars that Canada's pop-culture scene needed. Common was the handsome singing star of CBC Television's *Country Hoedown,* with a big car, a big house, and a mailbox that collected a thousand fan letters a week. Scott was the afternoon disc jockey at Calgary's CFCN Radio, voted by listeners as the most popular country-music announcer in western Canada. Both media-made celebrities, Common and Scott came to country music as city boys who preferred other musical genres. Lacking the enduring talent or the versatility that would have carried them into second careers once their style of Canadian culture became *passé,* they flared briefly like shooting stars and then disappeared. Both saw their lives darkened by failed marriages and alcoholism. And both ended their lives in their fifties, sadly and tragically in Calgary.

Common, perhaps the more tragic of the two because his life ended violently in suicide, was born to perform. At age eight, growing up in Toronto, he did unpaid radio commercials for *Liberty* magazine. At eleven, he sang on radio's *Microphone Moppets.* At twenty-one, he was one of the rising hopefuls on such talent shows as CBC Television's *Pick the Stars* and Arthur Godfrey's *Talent Scouts* in the United States. At the same time he worked for the Ford Motor Company in Oakville, Ontario, as a hydraulic engineer.

Common's big break came in 1955 when he caught the ear of producer Drew Crossan, who was preparing a thirteen-week summer-replacement series called *Country Hoedown* for CBC Television. "Do you know any country and western songs?" asked Crossan. "No," replied Common. "Go out and learn 'Wagon Wheels,'" said Crossan, "and I'll see you on Friday."

D'arcy Scott, at that point, was an up-and-coming star in the Calgary radio market. He had learned his microphone skills as a high school student, doing announcing duties at teen dances, and he started in commercial radio at age eighteen as a disc jockey with CKLN Radio in Nelson, British Columbia. The same year, 1951, he married Yvonne, his high school sweetheart, and together they had five children. They moved to Red Deer after a couple of years in Nelson and then on to Calgary where Scott hit the big time with CKXL Radio.

CKXL was a country-music station, and so Scott became a country-music disc jockey. It didn't matter that the music he really liked was the big-band swing of Count Basie and Lester Young. It only mattered that he was able to sell the music to country fans. Scott researched country music and became an expert. He talked about it on air as if he had been a fan of Hank Williams and Johnny Cash all his life. It was all a harmless fiction, and Scott was the kind of charming rogue who could pull it off.

Common, too, had to acquire a taste for country music once he realized it was going to be his key to a career in show business. But first he had to decide if, in fact, he really wanted to leave his job at Ford to do music full-time. "Ford was a good job with a future," he said. "It was a rough choice." He opted to learn "Wagon Wheels."

Common was signed, along with another young singer—nineteen-year-old Tommy Hunter of London, Ontario—to do thirteen weeks of *Hoedown* at one hundred dollars a week. Hunter, with his lanky frame, weathered face, and cowboy guitar, was hired to appeal to rural audiences who liked the songs of Wilf Carter and Hank

Snow. Pint-sized Common, with his smooth-skinned good looks, slicked-down dark hair, and domesticated brand of sex appeal, was expected to be a draw among urban viewers, particularly women. Before joining *Hoedown*, he had sung the pop songs of Pat Boone and Perry Como. Now he would become Canada's answer to Marty Robbins, singing such western sagas as "El Paso" and "The Ballad of the Alamo."

The formula worked. Tommy Common and Tommy Hunter became household names across Canada. *Country Hoedown* was booked as a regular series and, in its first full season, ranked among Canada's top ten television shows. Listeners of a Saint John, New Brunswick, radio station voted Common as their favourite Canadian singer. After a series of guest performances on other CBC variety shows, Common received the Liberty Award from Ed Sullivan for best male singer on Canadian television.

While Common gave Canadians his version of Marty Robbins, Scott gave his fans the real thing. Robbins was one of the many big-name performers Scott introduced to audiences through a series of Grand Ole Opry-style concerts that he promoted in tandem with his work as a radio announcer. "Another D'arcy Scott Attraction" at the Calgary Corral in 1957 meant that, for $1.75 to $2, paying customers could see a show featuring the likes of Johnny Cash, Carl Perkins, Wanda Jackson, the Tennessee Two Band, and "the pumping piano of Jerry Lee Lewis." The concerts never made money, but they served to keep Scott's profile as high as those of the stars he promoted.

As well as promoting music stars, Scott also endeared himself to local hopefuls by supporting their showbiz ambitions. He saw a sixteen-year-old country singer named Ray Griff playing at a high school dance and invited him over to the radio station to record his songs. A year later, Scott had Griff appearing at the Grand Ole Opry in Nashville and touring as the opening act for Johnny Horton.

Scott thrived as a country-music deejay. He moved from CKXL to CFCN, the most popular country-music station in Calgary, and became known as the "colonel of country music" when the state of Louisiana—for reasons that remain shrouded in radio myth—made him an honourary colonel in its militia. He was also known as

"D Dogies," a nickname given to him by the country singer Ferlin Huskey. He wore expensive western boots and hats and drove a big pink Oldsmobile.

The trappings of success for Common also included the fancy clothes and the big car—an elegant Chrysler Windsor—and he had one of Canada's first fan clubs, with mail surpassing one thousand letters a week. He moved into a spacious new Toronto home with his wife, Deeny, the former Doreen Stevens, and he took on the role of resident rascal and practical joker with the *Hoedown* gang. He sometimes hired strippers to make unexpected appearances during *Hoedown* rehearsals, a distraction that kept the weekly routine from getting too predictable as the show settled in for a long run on the national network.

For all his success and love of practical joking, though, Common never seemed entirely comfortable in his role as a *Hoedown* regular. He confessed his insecurities to a *Globe and Mail* reporter after *Hoedown* had been on the air for four years: "I'm not a western singer," he admitted. "I've always considered myself a pop singer. Perhaps there might be bigger opportunities elsewhere in making club dates."

To compound his feelings of insecurity, Common drew a blank whenever he tried to capitalize on his television success by seeking a recording contract. Though he co-owned a chain of Tommy Common's Teen Town record stores, he was never able to use them as a vehicle for his own talent. *Toronto Telegram* columnist Alex Barris suggested that Common's talent was the problem: "Whenever they're approached about recording Tommy's voice, the moguls of that branch of entertainment reply with characteristic cynicism (and I'm afraid equally characteristic disregard for the English language) that Tommy 'sings too good.'"

The insecurities led to drinking and the drinking led to driving infractions. In 1960, Common was charged with impaired driving and failing to remain at the scene of an accident when he hit a car parked on a Toronto street. The impaired charge was withdrawn, but he was convicted on the second charge and fined three hundred dollars. Four years later, he was fined two hundred dollars after his car struck a woman in a pedestrian crosswalk.

Common's insecurities grew when *Country Hoedown* was cancelled in 1965 and Tommy Hunter was invited to host his own show on the network. Common said bitterly that if he were nine inches taller—he was five-foot-seven, Hunter was six-foot-four—he would have been chosen to host the new program. But the reality was that the CBC wanted a show featuring a country-music star, and Common simply didn't fit the bill. *The Tommy Hunter Show* remained on the air for the next twenty-seven years.

Common underwent a number of personal changes, some for the worse, after he lost the *Hoedown* job. His marriage to Deeny, mother of his four children, ended in 1967 with a bitter fight over alimony. The following year, his brother Jim, depressed over a broken romance, asphyxiated himself in a garage. Jim's suicide left Common an emotional wreck. His began to drink more heavily and friends feared for his mental stability.

In 1970 Common married Patti Reid, daughter of a Bracebridge, Ontario, hotel owner, and he worked seasonally for her father as manager at an Ontario summer resort. He struggled to re-establish himself in the music business as a supper-club entertainer.

Scott was also struggling. The showbiz partying lifestyle had finally caught up with him, and at age thirty-seven he was out of radio and no longer promoting concerts. He left the airwaves and dropped out of sight. A few years later, Scott suffered a stroke. His marriage dissolved and he became increasingly reclusive. He lived on a disability pension and listened to his big-band albums. He moved into his mother's home and looked after her as her health declined. Ray Griff wrote and recorded a song, "D Dogies," to remind people of Scott's contribution. The refrain went: "The old town is missing its number one country deejay."

After eight years in showbiz limbo, Common returned to television in 1973 as the host of CBC's *It's a Musical World,* on location with a group of singing children. The show was a good fit for Common. After its first season the show was renewed and retitled *Tommy Common's Musical World.* It continued to build ratings for four years until 1977, when CBC programmers decided Common's style of performing was too hokey and abruptly cancelled the show. The network where he had once been the number one fan-mail draw dropped him for a second time. Discouraged, Common went back on the road. He was now forty-four, with less hair and more weight, but he felt he still had a future in show business.

Gail Taylor, a thirty-year-old redhead, entered Common's life when she asked him to play a club she was managing in Regina. Her marriage was in trouble and so was his. He divorced Patti and moved with Taylor to Calgary, where she had grown up. "Gaylor," as he nicknamed her, became his live-in girlfriend and business manager. But as nightclubs converted into discos, the bookings dried up. Common put away his tuxedo and began selling real estate with Gail. On the surface, he seemed content to be living a "normal" life, but he was deeply in debt—he even owed money to his eighty-one-year-old mother—and he was drinking more than ever.

In 1979, Taylor convinced Common to enter an alcoholism treatment centre in Calgary, and for a time his life improved. He pulled himself out of bankruptcy and landed a job as special assistant to Liberal senator Horace "Bud" Olson, who had been appointed minister of state for economic and regional development in Pierre Trudeau's cabinet. Olson was surprised that Common would want a job normally given to an energetic twenty-five-year-old, but his enthusiasm convinced the senator that Common was the right choice.

Common liked politics but not everyone in politics liked him. A Liberal party worker said he could be hostile and belligerent "even when he wasn't drinking." Common, in fact, gave up the bottle for three years while working for Olson, but he returned to drinking in February 1984 when John Turner won the Liberal leadership race and dropped Olson from his cabinet. Olson closed his Calgary office, and Common criss-crossed the country in a vain search for work. In August 1984, he tried unsuccessfully for the Liberal nomination in Calgary's Bow River riding. He thought he had a following but became painfully aware of just how small it was when he lost the nomination by a big margin to former Edmonton alderman Charles Tanner.

By the time Common finally found a job, as co-coordinator of Calgary's anti-vandalism program at a salary of thirty thousand dollars a year, his self-esteem was shattered. He plunged into the work with characteristic enthusiasm, but at home he alternated between moods of violence and despair. His two cars were repossessed and his debts mounted. He became obsessed with repaying his financial obligation to his aging mother, although his salary would not allow him to do so. He disappeared from home for days at a time. When he returned, he became uncontrollably drunk and police were called to the house to calm him down.

In May 1985, Common took an overdose of tranquilizers. Taylor, at the end of her tether, suggested he get help and asked him to move out. He checked himself into the psychiatric ward of Calgary's Holy Cross Hospital and was diagnosed a manic-depressive. He remained in the hospital for three weeks, maintaining a semblance of normalcy by going to work each morning on a day pass. As soon as he was discharged, he started drinking again. He wasn't welcome at home, so he stayed with a male friend who owned a sizable handgun collection.

On June 3, Common and Taylor were supposed to meet for lunch, but he telephoned just before noon to say he was going to Heritage Park to kill himself. Two hours later Taylor received a frightened call from her daughter Lisa, who was home in bed with the flu. Common had driven his car into the backyard and was trying to connect a clothes dryer hose to the exhaust pipe. Then he stormed around the yard, hurled a garden rake through a kitchen window, and climbed inside. He threatened to burn to death the family's dog, scatter the ashes around the house, and then burn down the house. Police were on the scene within minutes. Common was arrested and charged with breaking and entering.

The story made headlines across Canada. Common was suspended without pay from his job with the city. "How," he asked plaintively, "can a man break into his own house?" Taylor tried to assure him that he wouldn't be jailed for the offence, but he became increasingly despondent. He began leaving messages for her at work saying, "Tommy Common passed away two hours ago."

From then on, said Taylor, "It was like watching someone's life slip through an hourglass and there's nothing you can do." Common frequently shadowed her in the obsessive belief that she was being unfaithful. In early August, he met her for dinner and menacingly handed her a silver bullet. "This is for you," he said. "You're dead." The next night they met again for dinner and Common sheepishly apologized.

On the morning of August 14, the day before he was to appear in court, Common's lawyer called to tell him that the provincial attorney general's department had reduced the break-and-enter charge to mischief. To the lawyer, Common sounded coherent and stable. He said he was due to meet for lunch with his roommate, to discuss starting a horse-boarding business together.

Common never made the lunch. He phoned a friend to complain that he was being persecuted by police, that more charges were being laid, and that a judge was out to get him. Then he drove to a Macleod Trail bar and drank half a bottle of rye, several Scotches, and some beer. When Taylor emerged from her house shortly before noon, she saw Common sitting behind the steering wheel of his roommate's blue 1983 GMC pickup truck, parked nose-to-nose with her car. As she turned the key in the ignition, Common pointed a Luger automatic, which he had taken from his roommate's gun collection, through the windshield at her face. "Don't start the car," he shouted.

Taylor switched off the ignition and opened the door to leave the vehicle. He shifted aim and fired a shot into the pavement. Then he put the gun to his head. She ran toward the house to call police. As she reached the doorstep, she heard a second shot. She didn't look back. "Tommy's got a gun," she told the emergency operator. "But please don't arrest him, just subdue him."

When police arrived, they found Common slumped across the seat with a 9 mm bullet in his right temple. "I thought he was acting," said Taylor. "He'd fooled us so many times before, I couldn't believe he'd done it. I just couldn't believe it."

His suicide, as writer Alan Hustak has observed, seemed perhaps inevitable in light of the alcoholism and paranoia that followed his second rejection by the CBC. Born to perform, Common received what he saw as a death sentence when the opportunity to sing on television was taken away from him. "He was one of Canada's first television singing stars, undermined by the very people who gave him a public profile," wrote Hustak in an article for *Calgary* magazine.

Not one of those CBC people bothered to send flowers to Common's funeral, or even a message of condolence.

Common was fifty-one when he took his own life on August 14, 1985. The same year, D'arcy Scott was inducted into the Alberta Country Music Hall of Fame. He had briefly tried for a comeback with a syndicated radio program out of Drumheller, but it went nowhere. He had lost his taste for country-music radio when he finally realized that for him it was never going to get any better than sitting behind a microphone with a stack of records that he didn't really like, trying to sell something that he didn't really believe in.

Scott died in June 1993 at age fifty-nine, a victim of bad diet, no exercise, and one too many wasted days and wasted nights. Ray Griff faxed condolences from Nashville. "He was," said Griff, "the original innovator of country music deejays in Canada. He was also the best."

Dorothy Joudrie

Socialite

1935–2002

On January 21, 1995, Calgary police arrested fifty-nine-year-old Dorothy Joudrie and charged her with attempting to murder her estranged husband, Earl, a wealthy corporate executive, after shooting him six times with a small-calibre handgun. The subsequent criminal trial, which attracted reporters from across Canada, laid bare the sordid secrets of one Calgary's most prominent families. Behind a façade of domestic bliss, the couple had kept hidden for thirty-eight years the reality of a troubled marriage scarred by physical and emotional abuse and heavy drinking.

The Joudries had lived what a friend saw as "an absolutely ideal life" before the shooting that thrust them into the harsh glare of the media spotlight. They had started dating when both were attending Westglen High School in Edmonton during the early 1950s. Dorothy was fifteen and Earl was sixteen. Her parents, both schoolteachers, had raised Dorothy to believe that the ultimate destiny for a young woman was to marry and to marry well. Earl Joudrie came from working-class roots and believed that the role of a good wife was to be a chatelaine, looking after the household and supporting her husband as he advanced in his career. When they announced their engagement on Christmas Eve 1954, it seemed as if Dorothy's romantic dreams—and the expectations of her middle-class parents—had been fulfilled. She was finishing an education degree at the University of Alberta that would provide her with a profession until she started having children, and he was set to make a career for himself in the oil industry after he graduated from the U of A with a bachelor of arts degree.

They were married in August 1957. Dorothy taught for four years until the arrival of their adopted son, Neale, in the fall of 1961.

From then on, she remained at home while Earl pursued his career in the oil patch, initially as a landman and office manager for United Producing Company. They settled in Calgary, where their three other children—daughter Carolyn and sons Colin and Guy—were born. Dorothy dealt with the "daily things that happened with my children" and revelled in her role as wife and mother. "My family is the most important thing in my life," she said.

Earl quickly ascended the corporate ladder. By 1963, when he was twenty-nine, he had become Canadian division manager for Ashland Oil and Refining Company, a Kentucky-based oil giant. Two years later, he was named president and chief executive officer of Ashland Oil Canada. To friends and relatives, the Joudries seemed to have a glamorous and exciting life. They lived in an upscale Calgary neighbourhood, vacationed abroad, threw lavish parties, golfed, skied, played bridge, and socialized with important people.

But outward appearances were misleading. The marriage was troubled from the outset. Dorothy and Earl argued like any couple, but sometimes their arguments turned violent. "We did have what you would call a volatile relationship," testified Dorothy at her trial, describing an incident early in their marriage in which Earl slammed her against a wall and she retaliated by throwing a high-heeled shoe at him while he retreated behind a bedroom door. In a more serious incident, she said, he elbowed her in the face and broke her nose. Dorothy said she never told anyone about these violent episodes "because I thought it was my fault." She didn't even confide in her parents "because I didn't want Earl to look bad." Earl acknowledged in court that their arguments sometimes went from "angry voices, to pushing and shoving, to my striking her" but added, "sometimes she can be violent. So this wasn't a one-way street this pushing and shoving going on."

The problems were kept secret from family and friends, including the fact that in May 1971 Earl was diagnosed with Hodgkin's disease, a form of lymphoma. He underwent an experimental treatment at Stanford University Medical Center in California while Dorothy commuted back and forth and pretended to her parents that everything was fine. When Earl recovered, he moved the family and the head office of Ashland Canada from Calgary to Toronto where, said

Dorothy, the "most arguments and the most violence" occurred. The family's live-in nanny, Elizabeth Griffiths, testified, "I saw Earl Joudrie hitting Dorothy Joudrie on numerous occasions," including one occasion when the children were present and "I was afraid he would kill her." Griffiths phoned the police, but when they arrived "Dorothy would not lay charges. I couldn't believe it."

The violence came to a head in 1978, two years after Earl accepted a position as senior vice-president and group operating officer at Ashland's headquarters in Kentucky. Earl testified that he couldn't remember how the fight started, "but it progressed to the point where she was struck and her ribs were—I mean, proven later to be sore. I don't think they were broken, but she was certainly hurt." He added that the incident shocked both of them into realizing that things had to change. "I agreed that I would not, you know, do that, and Dorothy agreed that she would try somehow to be somewhat less provocative and back the hell off on occasion. And I think we stuck to that pretty well." Although he was in line for another promotion, Earl decided it would be best to resign and move back to Calgary for the sake of the marriage.

The physical abuse stopped after the Joudries returned to Calgary, where Earl soon landed the top jobs at both Nu-West Homes and Voyager Petroleums, followed by later senior appointments with Dome Canada, Gulf Canada, and Canadian Tire. But, said Dorothy, "we had arguments and fights and throwing of things and holes in the wall and taking lamps and throwing them across the room." They attended marriage counselling sessions during the mid-1980s, during which time Dorothy acknowledged that she had a drinking problem.

Earl moved into his own apartment in Calgary in October 1989. The next year, Dorothy left the family home and bought a luxury condominium in the comfortable Bearspaw district northwest of Calgary. A legal separation was drawn up providing Dorothy with a settlement of $1.9 million. The Joudries continued to appear in public as husband and wife until July 1991, when Earl approached Dorothy with three possible "scenarios." In one, he could quit work, travel, play golf, and "just enjoy life." In the second, they could sell their big ranch house on the western outskirts of Calgary, find an apartment in the city and a less demanding job for him, and try to start over again. In the third, he could accept a "new, fantastic" job as chairman of the board of Algoma Steel, which would mean his moving back to Toronto. Dorothy immediately knew which option Earl wanted.

"If you take that scenario, do you have any room in your life for me?" she asked. "No," he replied. A few weeks later, his secretary called to tell Dorothy that Earl had moved to Toronto. Two years after that, Earl phoned Dorothy to say he was "moving in" with her second cousin, Lynn Manning, who was eight years Dorothy's junior and had once babysat the Joudrie children. Earl and Lynn had been seeing one another socially since Earl left Calgary in August 1991.

Earl and Dorothy continued to maintain occasional contact after Earl moved to Toronto. He sent her a Christmas card and gift in 1991 that "made me think maybe he did want to come back" and a birthday card in 1993 that led her to believe "he still cares." In 1994, she finally accepted that the marriage was over, and "I told him I would give him a divorce. I did tell him that."

The shooting occurred on a Saturday morning in January 1995 when Earl came to Calgary and stopped off at Dorothy's condominium, at her invitation, to pick up some family papers and mementoes and discuss their impending divorce. After what both described as a "quiet" conversation over coffee, during which Earl confirmed that, yes, he still wanted a divorce, she said "it's going to be easier for you than it is for me because you've got somebody and I'm all alone." He was about to leave the house through the garage— she had asked that he enter and exit that way—when he felt the first bullet hit him in the back. After five more shots, he lay bleeding on the garage floor with seven wounds to the shoulder, back, and thighs, a broken right arm, and a collapsed lung. "Why don't you sit down and talk to me?" he said. "How long is it going to take you to die?" she replied. "The thing about Lynn isn't what you think," he said. "If you help me, I'll try to help you." A few moments later, she dialled 911.

Dorothy was charged with attempted murder, aggravated assault, and illegal use of a handgun, pleading not guilty to all three charges. The preliminary hearing was held in October 1995, nine months after the shooting, and the trial started on April 22, 1996, before a jury of eleven women and one man. The Crown prosecutor, Jerry Selinger, told the jury he would prove that the impending divorce had triggered Dorothy's rage and her "dastardly deed." Defence lawyer Noel O'Brien countered that the effects of alcoholism and living with physical and emotional abuse had caused Dorothy to surrender her voluntary judgment and behaviour, allowing her to act out in a robotic way, in what psychiatrists call a "dissociative" state, or what the lawyers call "automatism." It was an unusual and risky defence, rarely used successfully in Canada.

Two of the Joudrie children, youngest son Guy and daughter Carolyn, testified for the prosecution, describing a history of "yelling and screaming" and "physical confrontations" between their parents, which could begin over something as innocuous as a game of bridge. Guy testified that his mother drank from morning to night "seven days a week" and Carolyn said she preferred to talk with Dorothy on the telephone in the mornings because, by late afternoon, she seemed forgetful and would repeat herself. Dorothy acknowledged that she had started drinking to overcome her loneliness during the periods when Earl was absent on business trips, and that after he moved out in 1989 "I definitely was misusing alcohol and I was pouring drinks by myself at home." She added that during a twenty-eight-day stay at the Betty Ford Center in California, after the shooting, she learned that "I am an alcoholic" and now was "dealing with that daily, one day at a time."

Dorothy testified that she had bought the handgun, a .25-calibre semi-automatic Beretta, as protection for herself in Arizona, where she had a winter home, and had unintentionally brought it to Calgary, fully loaded, under the front seat of her car. She found the gun again in May 1994 when she was cleaning out the car before selling it. She said she stashed the gun in her bedroom dresser, intending to take it back to Phoenix on her next trip. When prosecutor Selinger suggested that she planned the shooting from the time she brought the gun to Calgary, Dorothy said, "I disagree with you completely." She said that while she remembered the conversations with Earl immediately before and after the shooting, she had no recollection of the actual shooting itself. She had poured herself a stiff drink before his arrival because, she said, when she was with Earl she was "pretty nervous."

Two psychiatrists testified for the defence, saying that Dorothy was in a dissociative state at the time of the shooting, which means that she would have no conscious awareness that shooting a gun was wrong in a legal sense. They said she was unlikely to repeat the behaviour if she dealt with the "massive denial" of her real-life situation and stopped drinking. The Crown's rebuttal witness, Dr. Julio Arboleda-Flores, surprised the courtroom spectators by saying he agreed with the defence experts about Dorothy's automatism. But he disagreed with their conclusion that a recurrence of trouble was unlikely. "Fifty per cent of murders are committed by people who are drunk," he said. The jury deliberated for twenty-one hours before reaching a verdict that Dorothy had "committed the acts alleged against her, but is not criminally responsible on account of a mental disorder." Defence lawyer O'Brien asked that the verdict be recorded as "not guilty," but the judge, Arthur Lutz, said the entry would be as the jury rendered it. He directed that Dorothy be sent to the Alberta Hospital psychiatric facility near Edmonton for an indefinite period of psychiatric assessment.

Earl's reaction to the verdict was guarded. "I presume the court will ensure that Dorothy receives proper care and treatment," he said. Two months after the trial, he married Lynn Manning in a private ceremony in Toronto. Media reports characterized Dorothy as a wealthy Calgary socialite who, because of her money, walked away with what one columnist called "the proverbial slap on the wrist." "If Dorothy Joudrie wasn't responsible for her act, then the government must be," said one headline. "A rich woman shoots her husband six times and gets a complete discharge," said broadcaster Hana Gartner on CBC Television's *The National Magazine*. "You could understand how this would enrage a community and make cynics say there is no justice." Defence lawyer O'Brien acknowledged that Dorothy had "enough wealth to enable her to afford the necessary medical assessments required to advance an extremely complicated defence." But, he added, she did not "buy" justice. "She was in a financial position to obtain the type of justice every citizen of this country should be able to get."

Dorothy spent five months in the Alberta Hospital, a place she described as a "gulag," and when she was released, initially on condition that she undergo further counselling for alcoholism, she said it was because "I had the money to fight the system." Others were doomed to stay in the hospital indefinitely, she said. "They didn't have the fifty thousand dollars I paid for outside psychiatrists and other doctors who could prove I wasn't a threat to society." She was granted an absolute discharge in October 1998 and freed from any further involvement with the hospital. She had been treated for Graves' disease (a thyroid disorder) and lymphatic cancer, and said she was looking forward to resuming her charity work, her golf and bridge, and "trying to make a difference with others less fortunate than myself."

In one of her last media interviews, in March 2000, Dorothy told the *National Post* that, thanks to her crusading efforts, two patients she met in the Alberta Hospital had won their freedom. She had lost friends because of what she called "this dreadful business," three of her four children still weren't talking to her, and she and Earl no longer had any contact with one another. "It's been horrible for everyone," she said. "It's such a sad, sad story, me and Earl. That we couldn't make it to our retirement." She had come from "an era that thought marriage should remain as a marriage, and I worked very hard and I loved my husband."

Dorothy Joudrie died at age sixty-six in February 2002 after succumbing to liver and kidney failure. "She had a number of demons that she fought for so long. The alcoholism was a major problem in her life which led to significant issues," lawyer O'Brien told the *Calgary Herald*. "Dorothy was always vilified in the press in many respects, but those who knew her—and I think I knew her very well, probably better than anyone—knew she certainly had a big heart." She had finally made peace with her four children, but she never made peace with her ex-husband.

Toto Miller

East Kootenay mayor and separatist

1944–1996

Toto Miller never did become an Albertan, but for a while there in 1991—when he was serving as mayor in the small coal-mining community of Sparwood, British Columbia—it seemed like an awfully good idea to him. In fact, he wanted his entire East Kootenay corner of southeastern B.C. to become part of Alberta. "I think it would be neat," he said when an Alberta member of the legislative assembly, Nick Taylor, proposed that residents of the area hold a referendum on the matter. "A lot of people in this area already do their major shopping and hospital visits to Lethbridge and Calgary," said Miller. "They may give their hearts to B.C. but their wallets go to Alberta—the land of no sales tax."

The first rumblings of separatist discontent from the area had been heard as far back as 1954. Feeling isolated from the provincial capital of Victoria and the business centre of Vancouver, the East Kootenay region's residents told reporters that they felt economically, socially, and culturally aligned with the Crowsnest Pass coal-mining communities of Coleman, Blairmore, and Bellevue, on the Alberta side of the provincial boundary. Heck, they even shared the same time zone as Alberta; Vancouver and Victoria were one hour behind.

The separatist movement gathered momentum for a short time in 1974 when the area encompassing Sparwood, Fernie, and adjoining communities was—due to a provincial cartographer's carelessness—omitted from a B.C. road map prepared especially for Expo '74 in Spokane, Washington. The mayor of Fernie responded by issuing a call for the region's secession from British Columbia. "We're not kidding," he told a Calgary newspaper. "We want to join Alberta—if Premier Lougheed will have us." Lougheed responded by saying jokingly that "somehow or other, I think, in this enterprising province of course, we may be able to handle a seventy-sixth constituency."

The 1974 separatist initiative finally fizzled when the B.C. government issued an apology over the map mix-up. The Fernie board of trade chopped up its wooden "Welcome to Alberta" highway sign and used it for firewood. Things stayed like that until 1991, when MLA Taylor rekindled the separatist embers by saying the area's residents should vote on whether to remain with British Columbia or amalgamate with Alberta. "Victoria is a long ways away," said Taylor. "I think Alberta would be the choice."

Several area residents voiced support for Taylor's proposal. Among them was Sparwood's mayor, Toto Miller, a convenience store operator with a reputation for grabbing headlines. "For many years there has been a real feeling of neglect here," said Miller.

Miller had felt that sense of neglect from the time he first arrived in Sparwood in 1977. Born in Rennes, France, the son of French and Polish parents, he was christened Otthon Edouard Charles—Otto for short. His family immigrated to Canada in 1949, when he was five. "I was deported and my family followed," he joked later. They settled in Merritt, B.C., where his parents—conscious of postwar anti-German sentiment—changed his German-sounding first name from Otto to Toto.

Miller lived in Merritt until he finished high school and then moved to Vancouver to spend eight years collecting degrees and certificates in various disciplines. He worked as a freelance journalist, broadcaster, and screenwriter, and eventually fell into a discipline that he hadn't studied, education. He worked as a substitute teacher at a Burnaby high school for a year and then returned to Merritt, where he taught English for a year.

He continued to teach for two more years after he moved to Sparwood with his wife and two daughters in 1977. Sparwood, with a population of four thousand, was then a young town. It had been created as an instant community in 1966 to accommodate miners and their families after the historic B.C. mining towns of Michel, Natal, and Middletown were razed. Miller quit teaching after he bought a newsstand and lottery-ticket agency in the town's main shopping mall and renamed it Toto's Place. During that same period, he became involved in local service clubs and in a political action committee that was lobbying for improvements to municipal services.

By the early 1980s, Miller was serving as a school board trustee. His standard approach at board meetings, as a female colleague recalled, was to be confrontational: "Toto performed as only Toto could, arriving for meetings late, disrupting meetings, getting his trustee colleagues totally upset, and trading insults." She added that his apparent purpose was to force other trustees to consider whether or not they were acting in the best interests of the children. "Often controversial, he was respected by some and hated by others," she said. "But he was totally committed to good education."

In 1983, after serving one term as alderman, Miller ran successfully for mayor. During interviews with out-of-town reporters, he talked about the frustrations of being so far away from Victoria and Ottawa. Edmonton, he noted wryly, was much closer than Victoria. Calgary was even closer. "Basically, we have to live with neglect," he said. "We'd like the politicians to come out here once in a while and say 'Hi!' They shouldn't just come here at election time with their promises." Besides, he added, the promises were usually empty anyhow. "We've been cheated and lied to so often we're cynical." As examples, he pointed to the provincial government dragging its feet on building a needed vocational school for his area, and the federal government restricting imports of Japanese cars—which negatively affected the amount of coal that Sparwood could ship to Japan for use in that country's thermal electric plants.

His concerns with Victoria and Ottawa aside, Miller became known in Sparwood as a people's mayor who took a personal interest in the concerns of his community and his constituents. "You have to be out there with the people," he said. "You have to walk with the people, listen to family situations, hear about what they have to say. It's a whole community, it's like a family."

Miller ran for re-election in 1986, but personal troubles got in the way. His wife divorced him and he lost custody of their children. He ran up a large business debt and began drinking heavily, which was especially dangerous for Miller because he suffered from chronic diabetes to the point of being almost blind. He lost the election by eight votes to a United Church minister, Colin Curties. "Let's face it, the public had a right to kick my ass," Miller said afterwards. "I wasn't paying attention." The alcohol had become an escape for him, he acknowledged. "The walls tend to close in fast. The first place that draws you is a pub."

After losing the election, he suffered another setback when a woman he was involved with was killed along with her children in a car accident near Pincher Creek. The support of the community helped him through those dark days, he said. "The public was there behind me, nothing to do with politics," he said. "The only way to judge your friends is when they're there at your lowest point."

Miller made his comeback in 1988, defeating Reverend Curties by eighty-eight votes and reclaiming the mayor's chair for life. Because the citizens had supported him through the rough times, he said he would combine the job of mayor with that of social worker and counsellor. "The role of a mayor is the role of a good friend," he said. "I'll go for lunch at noon and quite often leave at four o'clock. It's not just because I'm the mayor, it's because I'm Toto. I carry the burden for a lot of people."

As he looked out for his fellow citizens, so too did they look out for him. His lunch companions would butt out his smouldering cigarettes as he ate and help him whenever he suffered a diabetic seizure. This happened fairly regularly because Miller invariably forgot to take his medication.

Miller's efforts to turn his people into Albertans came to naught. The 1991 referendum proposal never got off the ground. Government officials pointed out that adjusting provincial boundaries involved much more than redrawing the map and putting a sign on the highway. Matters such as provincial mineral rights and public utility transfers would have to be sorted out first.

In 1993, Miller's penchant for grabbing headlines brought him coverage in the British Columbia newspapers, when he placed a personal advertisement in the *Vancouver Province* offering to marry Prime Minister Kim Campbell. "Single up-valley mayor seeking loving companionship of single Canadian prime minister," said the ad. "Object: politics and her pension." He told reporters jokingly that he was the "sex symbol of the Elk Valley" and that he didn't want romance, "just a loving political relationship." "I haven't heard back from her, but I'm waiting anxiously," he said. He added that aside from giving people a laugh, the object of the ad was to draw some attention to the problems of Sparwood, which had been hit hard economically by the closing of the coal mines.

Miller never did hear back from Campbell. When she became the host of a talk show on a Vancouver radio station in August 1995, Miller tried phoning her but couldn't get on the air. "I'm disappointed, but I'm still available, and she can come to Sparwood any time," he told reporters.

Miller died a year later, in August 1996, of a massive heart attack at his Sparwood home. He was fifty-two, still single, and still a British Columbian. The mayor who would be Albertan had served for eleven of the previous thirteen years. "He could become a real pain in the butt if things went the wrong way," said the editorial in the *Elk Valley Miner*. "But despite that, or maybe because of it, he was a well-respected politician." A month after he died, a letter came to his office from B.C. Liberal leader Gordon Campbell that served to prove what Miller had been saying all along about Victoria politicians not really knowing or caring much about Sparwood. "It was great to see you at the Union of B.C. Municipalities convention in September," wrote Campbell, who later became premier of British Columbia. The members of Sparwood town council were not amused.

Owen "Blue Blazer" Hart

Professional wrestler

1965–1999

The conventional knock against professional wrestling is that it is fake—an elaborate televised charade in which the actors pretend to do violence to one another, with no real threat to life or limb. But there was nothing fake about the groin injury that wrestler Owen Hart sustained in 1992 when he seriously considered quitting the ring and getting into a safer line of work. Nor, needless to say, was there anything fake about the freak accident that took his life at a Kansas City wrestling event in 1999, when he was about to descend by cable from the arena ceiling as though lowered from heaven to do battle with evil.

The baby of Calgary's famed wrestling Hart clan, Owen was undoubtedly born to wrestle, albeit reluctantly at first. His father, Stu, wrestled for more than four decades and was the founder of Stampede Wrestling, a Calgary-based regional circuit that flourished before the World Wrestling Federation (now called World Wrestling Entertainment, after a legal battle with the World Wildlife Fund) started buying up small circuits and making local promoters redundant. Six of Owen's seven brothers became involved in pro wrestling, either inside the ring or out. Three of his four sisters married pro wrestlers. The youngest, Diana, became part of the wrestling scene in a scripted scenario that had her supposedly torn between supporting her husband, Davey Boy Smith, and her older brother, Bret "the Hitman" Hart, as the pair wrestled in London for a WWF championship belt. "She sat close to tears at ringside," reported the *Daily Mirror.*

Owen, born in May 1965, grew up in a household described by his sister Diana (two years older), as anything but normal. "How many kids can count Andre the Giant (seven-foot-four and 450 pounds) as one of their babysitters?" Their home was a Victorian mansion on Calgary's outskirts that had been an orphanage during the 1920s and was surrounded by thirty-five acres of weeds. Stu Hart drove the kids to school in a used airport-limousine Cadillac. Terrible Ted, a grizzly bear that wrestled humans, slept under the front porch. Frequent visitors to the home included wrestlers with such names as the Great Antonio, Sweet Daddy Siki, the Dynamite Kid, Bad News Allen, Abdullah the Butcher, and the two McGuire brothers, Billy and Benny, who together weighed close to fifteen hundred pounds and were listed in the *Guinness Book of World Records* as "the world's heaviest twins."

Like his brothers, Owen learned to wrestle in a training ring in the ten-thousand-square-foot family basement, nicknamed "the dungeon" because it was dark and claustrophobic, with rusty ceiling pipes and clammy walls. His father, Stu, referred to Owen and his sister Diana as "my little blonde palominos" because, like the horse of that name, they had golden tans and white manes. Of all his twelve children, said Stu, Owen and Diana had the most to offer in terms of athletic ability. "I remember them doing back flips and front flips right in my living room," he said. "I was so proud of them, especially because they were self-taught."

Owen was the joker of the family, a gifted actor who could impersonate people so effectively on the phone that he never failed to fool his listeners. It seemed like good training for a sports-entertainment career where he would often find himself participating in what the industry coyly calls "predetermined matches," that is, choreographed wrestling matches where the outcome is decided ahead of time, though the injuries are often real and bloody.

But for all his natural ability—both as an athlete and as a showman—Owen was not keen to follow his father and older brothers into wrestling. He wanted to be a gym teacher. "I wrestled only to appease my father," he revealed to *Saturday Night* magazine in 1993. "I was compelled to get into the ring. Once I started, there was the pressure of having the Hart name. I was expected to be good."

And he was good. Starting as an amateur in his teens, Owen wrestled with the University of Calgary Dinosaurs and won a Canadian collegiate championship. In May 1986, just after he turned twenty-one, he turned professional and joined the World Wrestling Federation as a character called "the Rocket." "I'm just the all-American, clean-cut, high-flying wrestler," he told an interviewer. "I don't have to paint my face."

The Rocket disappeared after a year, and Owen re-emerged as a masked mystery man, with no hint given to fans that he was a member of the famed Hart clan. In the backrooms of pro wrestling, it had been decided that the game should have just one Hart at a time and that was to be Owen's brother, Bret "the Hitman" Hart. The Hitman was a premier drawing card whose trademark move was "breaking" opponents' legs with chairs. *Alberta Report* magazine characterized him as "almost certainly the best-known Albertan on earth." In terms of world-famous Canadians, the Hitman was better known than actor Jim Carrey or singer Celine Dion. Owen was the anonymous "Blue Blazer," hidden by a mask and forbidden to reveal his identity. "It bothered me," said Owen, "because everyone knew who Bret was and was asking, 'Who is this guy in the mask?'"

As the Blue Blazer, Owen played a "good-guy" hero who urged fans to "say your prayers, take your vitamins, and drink your milk." The promoters planned to merchandize the Blue Blazer as a comic-book character, using the name to sell capes and masks. "But you couldn't tell if I was forty years old and balding or a young guy," said Owen. He was then twenty-three.

In 1992, Owen suffered an injury in the ring, and he began to wonder if it was all worth it. By then, he was married to the former Martha Patterson, a Calgary wrestling enthusiast he had known from high school. The injury occurred when he was performing an aerial manœuvre off the top rope and received a head butt to the groin. "I had to finish the match because it was on live TV, but I spent a week in hospital. I almost had to lose a testicle. I had just got married and wanted to start a family. It put into perspective the risks that I was taking."

Owen continued to wrestle anonymously as the Blue Blazer, then quit the WWF to wrestle in Japan and Europe under his own name. When he returned to the WWF, he was cast again in his original role as Owen "the Rocket" Hart, an acrobatic muscleman who did back flips and gymnastics and who harboured a grudge against his brother, the Hitman, who enjoyed greater fame and made much more money.

Whether the grudge was real or feigned hardly mattered. Their public feuding started during tag-team matches in Boston and Hartford, and culminated in a March 1994 bout between the two brothers in front of a sold-out crowd at New York's Madison Square Garden. Owen won the match and told the audience, with characteristic wrestling-industry hyperbole, that he was "the best there is, the best there was, and the best there will ever be." It was all a buildup for the inevitable return match.

Owen wasn't keen on making a career out of wrestling his own brother, but the WWF bosses liked the commercial potential of this latter-day Cain and Abel matchup. They scheduled the rematch for Calgary, with Bret's WWF championship title on the line. "They were saying we can't miss this opportunity," said Owen. As part of the promotion for the grudge rematch, Owen won a bout in Baltimore and had himself crowned King of Harts—a title his father had adopted in the 1940s.

To nobody's surprise, Owen lost the rematch. Bret retained his WWF title and Owen told the television cameras he was "disowning" Calgary. It was all good for business, and it guaranteed that future battles between the brothers would draw big crowds. By then it seemed as if they really were estranged. Media speculation suggested as much when Owen chose to remain with the WWF after Bret jumped in 1997 to the rival World Championship Wrestling, owned by television tycoon Ted Turner.

While Owen enjoyed great success as a wrestler, winning several titles both as a solo performer and as a tag-team wrestler, he often told the media that he wanted to get out of the game for the sake of his wife and two young children. "My wife and kids have been compromised enough," he told *Slam* magazine in 1999, a few months before the accident that took his life. "I need to start focussing on my family and letting go of wrestling." As if to prove the point, he subsequently took part in a WWF match where he "broke" an opponent's neck and afterwards claimed to be so distraught that he planned to retire from wrestling. But when the Blue Blazer character of his early career made a return to the ring in April 1999, fans realized that the "retirement" was just another WWF storyline. The gimmick in each match was for the Blazer's opponent to try and unmask him and "prove" he really was Owen Hart.

Although the fatal accident took place in an arena filled with eighteen thousand people, no one actually witnessed the harness failure that precipitated Owen's six-storey fall because his entrance was not due for several minutes. Nor did anyone immediately appreciate the chilling reality of what they were watching when paramedics and police attended to Owen, because ambulances and emergency workers are commonly featured in WWF storylines.

Owen's wife, Martha, sued the WWF for negligence and received a settlement of U.S. $18 million. The WWF indicated it would pursue its own lawsuit against the company that made the equipment used during the deadly stunt. Some WWF officials suggested that the accident might serve to tone down the garish histrionics and make television wrestling safer, but others in the sport disagreed. "Wrestling is just going to grow bigger and bigger," predicted Ted Annis, Owen's wrestling nephew, in a November 1999 interview with *Spank* magazine. "You watch—they're just going to do more crazy stuff." That same month, a face-painted professional wrestler named Sting was featured on pay-per-view television performing the same cable-descent stunt that had sent Owen to his death.

Afterword

My thanks to the following authors for writing the books that supported my storytelling in *Scoundrels and Scallywags: Characters from Alberta's Past*.

Audrey Andrews for *Be Good, Sweet Maid: The Trials of Dorothy Joudrie*; James Henry "Blackie" Audett for *Rap Sheet: My Life Story*; William Peter Baergen for *The Ku Klux Klan in Central Alberta*; Lynn Bowen for *Muddling Through: The Remarkable Story of the Barr Colonists*; Mary-Jo Burles for *First and Second Kings, Maurice and Harold*; Jock Carpenter for *The Bootlegger's Bride*; Anthony Walcott Cashman for *The Best Edmonton Stories*; Jack Dunn for *The Alberta Field Force of 1885*; Franklin Foster for *John E. Brownlee: A Biography*; Peter Foster for *The Blue-eyed Sheiks: The Canadian Oil Establishment*; Margaret Gilkes for *Calgary's Finest*; James H. Gray for *Red Lights on the Prairies*, *A Brand of its Own: The 100 Year History of the Calgary Exhibition and Stampede*, and *Talk to My Lawyer*; Diana Hart and Kirstie McLellan for *Under the Mat: Inside Wrestling's Greatest Family*; Ted Hart for *Ain't It Hell: Bill Peyto's Mountain Journal*; Leroy Victor Kelly and Hugh A. Dempsey for *North With Peace River Jim*; Donna Livingstone for *The Cowboy Spirit: Guy Weadick and the Calgary Stampede*; Grant MacEwan for *Fifty Mighty Men*, *Mighty Women*, *Calgary Cavalcade: From Fort to Fortune*, and *He Left Them Laughing When He Said Good-bye: The Life and Times of Frontier Lawyer Paddy Nolan*; James G. MacGregor for *John Rowand: Czar of the Prairies* and *The Land of Twelve Foot Davis: A History of the Peace River Country*; Murray Malcolm for *The Pursuit of Ernest Cashel*; Nancy Millar for *Remember Me As You Pass By: Stories from Prairie Graveyards*; Jack Peach for *Thanks for the Memories*; Helen Evans Reid for *All Silent, All Damned: The Search for Isaac Barr*; Philip Smith for *The Treasure-Seekers: The Men Who Built Home Oil*; Fred Stenson for *The Trade*; Roy St. George Stubbs for *Lawyers and Laymen of Western Canada*; Patrick Tivy for *Calgary Stampede and the Canadian West*; and Aritha van Herk for *Mavericks: An Incorrigible History of Alberta*.

Index

By Category

About the Author

PHOTO: BOB BLAKEY

Brian Brennan is an award-winning Irish-born Canadian author and musician who has lived and worked in Calgary since 1974. His recent books include *Alberta Originals: Stories of Albertans Who Made a Difference* and *Building a Province: 60 Alberta Lives,* both published by Fifth House Ltd., and *Máire Bhuí Ní Laoire: A Poet of her People* (The Collins Press), which was nominated for the Irish Times Literature Prize, 2001. Brennan is also co-author and co-editor of *Deadlines & Diversity: Journalism Ethics in a Changing World* (Fernwood). He has won two Western Magazine Awards and the national Hollobon Award for his journalism, and was an Ethics Fellow at the Poynter Institute in Florida.

Web site: http://www.brian-brennan.com